JACK ROLLIN's COMPLETE WORLD CUP GUIDE

The Author
Jack Rollin is the editor of *Rothmans Football Yearbook* and *The Guinness Book of Soccer Facts and Feats*. He writes a regular column for the *Sunday Telegraph* and contributes to *Radio Times*. For years he was BBC TV's top statistician and responsible for feeding their soccer commentators with information. He has also been the editor of *Soccer Star* magazine and the monthly *World Soccer*.

Acknowledgements

Official FIFA Report, World Cup Argentina '78; FIFA News; FIFA Technical Study 1970, 1974; History of the World Cup; Encyclopaedia of World Soccer; A–Z of World Soccer; England's World Cup Triumph 1966; World Cup Digest 1966; Koninklijke Nederlandsche Voetbalbond Handboek 1968; Football in Brazil 1978; Association Football 1960; Almanacco Illustrato del Calcio; Espana '82.

Conceived and produced by Pilot Productions Ltd.

First published in Great Britain by
Sphere Books Ltd 1982

TRADE
MARK

Set in Palatino by Preface Ltd of Salisbury
Printed and bound in Great Britain by
Richard Clay & Sons Ltd, Bungay.

JACK ROLLIN's
COMPLETE WORLD CUP GUIDE

SPHERE

SPHERE BOOKS LIMITED
30–32 Gray's Inn Road, London WC1X 8JL

Introduction

The idea of a World Cup emerged as long ago as 1904 when FIFA was formed, but it was not until 1930 that it became a reality and has since matured into the symbol of world soccer supremacy.

In the half century since it began the World Cup has grown in stature and this year, for the first time, the finals in Spain will have 24 teams competing for its prize.

But it began modestly enough. The Federation Internationale de Football Association (FIFA) was founded in Paris on 21 May 1904 by representatives of seven European countries: France, Belgium, Denmark, the Netherlands, Spain, Sweden and Switzerland.

Included in the statutes of what was to become the world governing body was a clause to the effect that FIFA alone would have the right to organise a world championship.

Membership gradually increased. Germany joined shortly afterwards; Austria, England and Italy the following year. By the end of the first World War there were 25 countries affiliated including Scotland and Wales admitted in 1910, and Northern Ireland a year later, plus Argentina, Brazil and Chile (as well as the USA) from the Americas.

In 1921 Jules Rimet a French lawyer became President of FIFA and the possibility of a World Cup came closer, though it took years of lengthy persuasion on his part to convince others to accept the idea.

His efforts were assisted in a practical way by Uruguay winning the Olympic Games football tournaments in 1924 and 1928. In May 1929 it was agreed that a World Cup competition would be held the following year.

Uruguay was an obvious choice as the host nation. They had proved their ability on the field and it coincided with the 100th anniversary of their independence as a country.

FIFA's membership then stood at 41, though England, Northern Ireland, Wales and Scotland had left the organisation for a second time and were ineligible for the inaugural competition.

The four had originally withdrawn after refusing to be associated with either Austria, Germany or Hungary, members of the axis nations in the first World War and they left for a second time over broken time payments to amateurs.

The trophy which was presented to the winners of the World Cup was a gold cup designed by Abel Lafleur a French sculptor and appropriately named after Jules Rimet himself.

After Brazil had won the cup three times in 1958, 1962 and 1970 they were allowed to retain it. In its place is the FIFA World Cup, designed by the Italian sculptor Silvio Gazamiga and made of solid gold 36 cm high and insured for £1.8 million.

The second World War interrupted the World Cup's cycle of four years and the competition did not resume until 1950, four years after the four British associations had re-joined FIFA.

The offices of FIFA were kept open during the period of hostilities from 1939–45 though the activities were practically nil and financial resources non-existent.

But the World Cup even transcended the war. Dr. Ottorino Barassi, late Vice President of FIFA, took the Jules Rimet Cup from the headquarters of the Italian F.A. then the holders, and hid it in a shoe box under his bed where it was never discovered by Nazi occupying troops. After the war he returned it safely to FIFA headquarters.

FIFA's membership now stands at 150 countries distributed in six Confederations. A record number of 108 of them entered the 1982 competition and the draw for the finals placed the 24 successful teams in six groups of four as follows:

Group 1	**Group 2**	**Group 3**
Italy	West Germany	Argentina
Poland	Algeria	Belgium
Peru	Chile	Hungary
Cameroon	Austria	El Salvador

Group 4	**Group 5**	**Group 6**
England	Spain	Brazil
France	Honduras	USSR
Czechoslovakia	Yugoslavia	Scotland
Kuwait	Northern Ireland	New Zealand

JACK ROLLIN, 1982

Contents

Explanatory notes

Statistical information about the respective 1982 finalists, taken from latest FIFA survey.

In the World Cup history section, figures in brackets after names: Smith (1) indicate goals scored. Figures in brackets are half-time scores. Penalty goals are denoted as: (pen.). F of Y is Footballer of the Year.

WC = World Cup.

World Cup Diary 1982

First phase

Date	Venue/ground	Match	Group
13 June	Barcelona (Nou Camp)	Argentina v Belgium	3
14 June	Vigo (Balaidos)	Italy v Poland	1
14 June	Seville (S. Pizjuan)	Brazil v USSR	6
15 June	La Coruna (Riazor)	Peru v Cameroon	1
15 June	Elche (Nuevo Estadio)	Hungary v El Salvador	3
15 June	Málaga (La Rosaleda)	Scotland v New Zealand	6
16 June	Gijon (El Molinon)	West Germany v Algeria	2
16 June	Bilbao (San Mames)	England v France	4
16 June	Valencia (Casanova)	Spain v Honduras	5
17 June	Oviedo (C. Tartiere)	Chile v Austria	2
17 June	Valladolid (Nuevo Zorrilla)	Czechoslovakia v Kuwait	4
17 June	Zaragoza (La Romareda)	Yugoslavia v N. Ireland	5
18 June	Vigo (Balaidos)	Italy v Peru	1
18 June	Alicante (Rico Perez)	Argentina v Hungary	3
18 June	Seville (B. Villamarin)	Brazil v Scotland	6
19 June	La Coruna (Riazor)	Poland v Cameroon	1
19 June	Elche (Nuevo Estadio)	Belgium v El Salvador	3
19 June	Málaga (La Rosaleda)	USSR v New Zealand	6
20 June	Gijon (El Molinon)	West Germany v Chile	2
20 June	Bilbao (San Mames)	England v Czechoslovakia	4
20 June	Valencia (Casanova)	Spain v Yugoslavia	5
21 June	Oviedo (C. Tartiere)	Algeria v Austria	2
21 June	Valladolid (Nuevo Zorrilla)	France v Kuwait	4
21 June	Zaragoza (La Romareda)	Honduras v N. Ireland	5
22 June	La Coruna (Riazor)	Peru v Poland	1
22 June	Elche (Nuevo Estadio)	Belgium v Hungary	3
22 June	Málaga (La Rosaleda)	USSR v Scotland	6
23 June	Vigo (Balaidos)	Italy v Cameroon	1
23 June	Alicante (Rico Perez)	Argentina v El Salvador	3
23 June	Seville (Villamarin)	Brazil v New Zealand	6
24 June	Oviedo (C. Tartiere)	Algeria v Chile	2
24 June	Valladolid (Nuevo Zorrilla)	France v Czechoslovakia	4
24 June	Zaragoza (La Romareda)	Honduras v Yugoslavia	5
25 June	Gijon (El Molinon)	West Germany v Austria	2
25 June	Bilbao (San Mames)	England v Kuwait	4
25 June	Valencia (Casanova)	Spain v N. Ireland	5

Squads include names of players likely to form nucleus of 22 selected prior to the finals in Spain in June.

Names appearing in brackets from the 1970 competition onwards denote players who appeared as substitutes.

International results 1982 up to end of February.

Brazilian and some Spanish players are listed under their playing names rather than their full title, e.g. Brazil's Zico (Arthur Antunes Coimbra).

Second phase

Each of sections A to D (see Chart right) are comprised of 3 teams. For the sake of convenient reference in our Diary, each team has been accorded a letter (denoting the section in which it appears) and a number (denoting its position within its section in the Chart right). So, for example, Winner Group 1 is described here as A1, and Winner Group 4 (will it be England?) is known as B2.

28 June	Madrid (Calderon)	D2 v D3
28 June	Barcelona (Nou Camp)	A1 v A2
29 June	Barcelona (Sarria)	C3 v C2
29 June	Madrid (Bernabeu)	B1 v B2
1 July	Madrid (Calderon)	D1 v Losers of D2 v D3
1 July	Barcelona (Nou Camp)	A3 v Losers of A1 v A2
2 July	Barcelona (Sarria)	C1 v Losers of C3 v C2
2 July	Barcelona (Bernabeu)	B3 v Losers of B1 v B2
4 July	Madrid (Calderon)	D1 v Winners of D2 v D3
4 July	Barcelona (Nou Camp)	A3 v Winners of A1, v A2
5 July	Barcelona (Sarria)	C1 v Winners of C3 v C2
5 July	Madrid (Bernabeu)	B3 v Winners of B1 v B2

Semi-finals

8 July	Barcelona (Nou Camp)	Winners Section A 2nd phase v Winners Section C 2nd phase
8 July	Seville (S. Pizjuan)	Winners Section B 2nd phase v Winners Section D 2nd phase

3rd/4th place match

10 July	Alicante (Rico Perez)	Semi-final losers

Final

11 July	Madrid (Bernabeu)	Semi-final winners

Test your wits and complete the brackets in the World Cup chart on page 9. It is interesting to note that neither England nor Northern Ireland will meet Scotland unless they advance beyond the semi-finals (a point that should make for a united front amongst British fans in Spain), and it's impossible for both Argentina and Brazil to play in the final on July 11.

The Way To The World Cup Final

First phase

*denotes top seeds

Group 1:
Italy*
Poland
Peru
Cameroon

Group 3:
Argentina*
Belgium
Hungary
El Salvador

Group 6:
Brazil*
USSR
Scotland
New Zealand

Group 2:
W. Germany*
Austria
Chile
Algeria

Group 4:
England*
France
Czechoslovakia
Kuwait

Group 5:
Spain*
Yugoslavia
N. Ireland
Honduras

Second phase

Section A:
Winner Group 1
A1 (POLAND)
Winner Group 3
A2 (BELGIUM)
Second Group 6
A3 (USSR)

Section C:
Winner Group 6
C1 (BRAZIL)
Second Group 3
C2 (ARGENTINA)
Second Group 1
C3 (ITALY)

Section B:
Winner Group 2
B1 (W. GERMANY)
Winner Group 4
B2 (ENGLAND)
Second Group 5
B3 (SPAIN)

Section D:
Winner Group 5
D1 (N. IRELAND)
Second Group 2
D2 (AUSTRIA)
Second Group 4
D3 (FRANCE)

Semi-finals

Winner Section A
(POLAND)
V
Winner Section C
(ITALY)

ITALY
The Final v
WEST GERMANY

Winner Section B
(W. GERMANY)
V
Winner Section D
(FRANCE)

Where Will They Play In Spain?

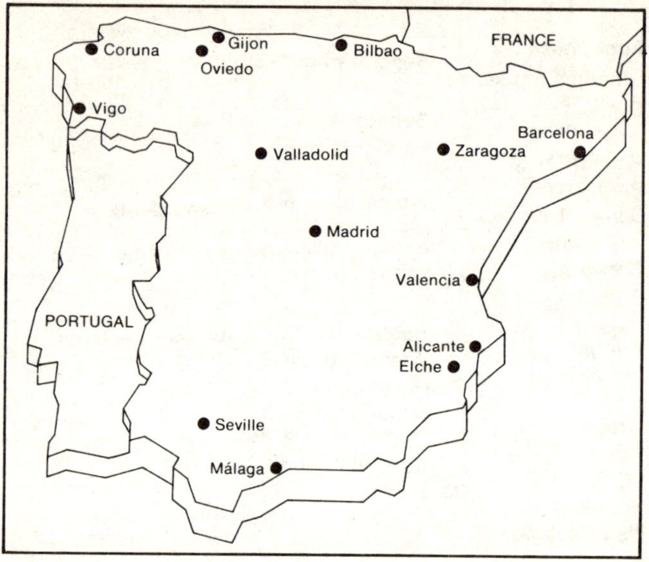

Average temperatures for June and July

Alicantę: Averages 272 sunny days a year; 22.7–25.5°C
Barcelona: Founded 2,000 years ago; 21.5–24.3°C
Bilbao: Port and industrial centre; 17.6–19.5°C
La Coruna: "City in which no one is a stranger"; 16.5°C constant
Elche: Agricultural and industrial area; 22.7–24.5°C
Gijon: Steel and mineral traffic; 16.0–18.0°C
Madrid: 4 million inhabitants; 531 sq. km; 20.6–24.2°C
Malaga: Tourist zone capital; 22.6–24.9°C
Oviedo: In area of unique beauty; 16.0–18.0°C
Seville: Noted for its cuisine; 21.2–24.1°C
Valencia: 68% relative humidity; 22.1–25.3°C
Valladolid: 692 metres above sea level; 18.0–22.0°C
Vigo: Thriving and aggressive city; 17.0°C constant
Zaragoza: Historically artistic centre; 19.2–23.5°C

Team-By-Team Information Files

ITALY Group 1, seeded

Formed: 1898
Joined FIFA: 1905
Clubs: 21,845
Teams: 22,132
Players: 833,564
Referees: 13,449
Div. 1 clubs: 16
Season: Sept–June
Colours: Blue shirts, white shorts, blue stockings
Change: White shirts, blue shorts, blue stockings

Tenth appearance in World Cup finals. Winners: 1934, 1938; Runners-up 1970; Fourth: 1978

1982 qualifying results:
Luxembourg (A) 2-0, (H) 1-0; Denmark (H) 2-0, (A) 1-3; Greece (A) 2-0, (H) 1-1; Yugoslavia (H) 2-0, (A) 1-1

Goalscorers:
Graziani 3, Bettega 2, Collovati 2, Conti 2, Antognoni, Cabrini, Scirea

Other 1981 results:
Uruguay (A) 0-2; Netherlands (N) 1-1 (both Copa de Oro, Uruguay); East Germany (H) 0-0; Bulgaria (H) 3-2

1982:
France (A) 0-2

Strengths:
Technically gifted players from defence-orientated environment

Weakness:
Conflict of domestic game with more flexible freedom of national side

STARS TO WATCH

Dino Zoff (Juventus). Reflexes still nimble at 40. Unspectacular but excels as a shot-stopper after years of goalkeeping behind crowded defences. 97 caps

Fulvio Collovati (AC Milan). Commanding physical presence. Excellent exponent of ultra-tight marking, catenaccio-style stopper centre-back. Age 25. 24 caps

Paolo Rossi (Juventus). Suspended for two years up to May 1982. Centre-forward aged 25. Pace, skill, popular appeal as a would-be prodigal son. 19 caps

SQUAD

Goalkeepers:
Dino Zoff, Ivano Bordon, Giovanni Galli

Defenders:
Claudio Gentile, Antonio Cabrini, Fulvio Collovati, Gaetano Scirea, Pietro Vierchowod, Giuseppe Baresi, Luciano Marangon, Franco Baresi

Midfield:
Marco Tardelli, Giuseppe Dossena, Giampiero Marini, Gabriele Oriali, Giancarlo Antognoni, Carlo Ancelotti, Bruno Conti

Forwards:
Domenico Marocchino, Francesco Graziani, Roberto Pruzzo, Roberto Bettega, Franco Selvaggi, Paolo Rossi, Alessandro Altobelli

Manager:
Enzo Bearzot (Italy). Age 54. Appointed 1977. Previously assistant

POLAND Group 1

Formed: 1919
Joined FIFA: 1923
Clubs: 5,334
Teams: 11,343
Players: 234,052
Referees: 7,160
Div. 1 clubs: 16
Season: Aug–Nov; Mar–June
Colours: White shirts, red shorts, white stockings
Change: Red shirts, white shorts, red stockings

Fourth appearance in World Cup finals. Third: 1974

1982 qualifying results:
Malta (A) 2-0, (H) 6-0; East Germany (H) 1-0, (A) 3-2

Goalscorers:
Smolarek 5, Boniek, Buncol, Iwan, Lipka, Majewski, Szarmach, Ziekanowski

Other 1981 results:
Japan (A) 2-0; Japan (A) 4-2; Japan (A) 4-1; Japan (A) 3-0; Rumania (A) 0-2; Eire (H) 3-0; West Germany (H) 0-2; Portugal (A) 0-2; Argentina (A) 2-1; Spain (H) 2-3

Strengths:
Versatility through players encouragement to train in all positions.

Weakness:
Winter training interruptions; few outstanding new players

STARS TO WATCH

Zbigniew Boniek (Widzew Lodz). Enthusiastic, accomplished powerhouse in midfield; brilliant if slightly erratic. Vitality and stamina abound. Age 25. 50 caps

Wlodzimierz Smolarek (Widzew Lodz). Poland's best discovery in the last four years. Quick, accurate attacker with persistence and direct approach. Age 24. 12 caps

Wladyslaw Zmuda (Widzew Lodz). Calm and commanding as a central defender in the stopper role. Sure-footed performer and consistent choice. 73 caps. Age 28

SQUAD

Goalkeepers:
Piotr Mowlik, Jozef Mlynarczyk, Jacek Kazimierski

Defenders:
Wladyslaw Zmuda, Pawel Janas, Waldemar Matysik, Jan Jalocha, Tadeusz Dolnik, Roman Geszlecht, Marek Dziuba

Midfield:
Andrzej Buncol, Wlodzimierz Ciolek, Zbigniew Boniek, Piotr Skrobowski, Janusz Kupcewicz, Roman Wojcicki, Stefan Majewski, Andrzej Iwan

Forwards:
Grzegorz Lato, Andrzej Szarmach, Miroslav Okonski, Andrzej Palasz, Dariusz Dziekanowski, Wlodzimierz Smolarek, Krzysztof Baran

Manager:
Antoni Piechniczek (Poland). Age 40. Appointed 1981. Former club manager

PERU Group 1

Formed: 1922
Joined FIFA: 1922
Clubs: 6,158
Teams: 6,958
Players: 139,360
Referees: 2,316
Div. 1 clubs: 16
Season: Apr–Dec
Colours: All white
Change: Red shirts, white shorts, white stockings

Fourth appearance in World Cup finals

1982 qualifying results:
Colombia (A) 1-1, (H) 2-0; Uruguay (A) 2-1, (H) 0-0

Goalscorers:
La Rosa 2, Uribe 2, Barbadillo

Other 1981 results:
Czechoslovakia (H) 1-3; Bulgaria (H) 1-2; Chile (A) 0-3; Chile (H) 1-2

Strengths:
Shrewdly coached to play at their own, slower pace

Weakness:
Lack of top European opposition; unused to concentration of matches

STARS TO WATCH

Teofilo Cubillas (Fort Lauderdale, USA). Elegant 1970 left-winger of precise promise; now matured in midfield and schemer-in-chief with tactical sense. 54 caps. Age 32

Cesar Cueto (Nacional Medellin, Colombia). Developed fine understanding with Cubillas. Nine years experience with side. "The poet of the left foot". Age 28. 29 caps

Julio Uribe (Sporting Cristal). Sound attacking instincts; clever, two-footed scoring ability but often impetuous in front of goal. Age 24. 10 caps

SQUAD

Goalkeepers:
Ramon Quiroga, Eusebio Acasuzo, Jose Gonzalez Gonoza

Defenders:
Jaime Duarte, Hector Chumpitaz, Toribio Diaz, Roberto Rojas, Salvador Salguero, Oscar Artiaga

Midfield:
Jorge Olaechea, Cesar Cueto, Jose Velazquez, Julio Cesar Uribe, Teofilo Cubillas, Carlos Luis Reyna, German Leguia, Eduardo Malasquez, Juan Illescas

Forwards:
Geronimo Barbadillo, Juan Carlos Oblitas, Guillermo La Rosa, Freddy Ravello, Lisandro Navarro, Eduardo Rey Munoz, Alberto Gallardo, Percy Rojas, Richards Garrido, Raul Mejia, Juan Caballero, Alberto Castillo

Manager:
Elba de Padua Lima 'Tim' (Brazil). Age 72. Appointed 1981. Was 1938 World Cup player

CAMEROON Group 1

Formed: 1960
Joined FIFA: 1962
Clubs: 200
Teams: 264
Players: 9,328
Referees: 448
Div. 1 clubs: 16
Season: Oct–Aug

Colours: Green shirts, red shorts, yellow stockings
Change: Yellow shirts, green shorts, red stockings

First appearance in World Cup finals

1982 qualifying results:
Malawi (H) 3-0, (A) 1-1; Zimbabwe (H) 2-0, (A) 0-1; Zaire (A) 0-1, (H) 6-1; Morocco (A) 2-0, (H) 2-1

Goalscorers:
Milla 6, Aoudou 2, Kunde 2, M'bida 2, Onguene 2, Abega, Tokoto

Other 1981 results:
Togo (H) 4-0; Togo (A) 2-2; Tunisia (A) 1-1

1982:
Congo (H) 2-0

Strengths:
Enthusiasm and outstanding ability of a few players

Weakness:
Lack experience against first class opposition

STARS TO WATCH

Thomas N'Kono (Canon Yaounde). Supple, agile goalkeeper with fine positional sense. Former African F of Y. Over 60 appearances. Age 26. Africa's finest No. 1

Roger Milla (Bastia, France). Real name: Albert Miller. Fast forward, with control and finish in the air and on the ground. Attractive style. Age 29

Francois N'Doumbe Lea (Union Douala). Sweeper and captain of his club side who covers his defensive colleagues with expertise and precision. Age 27

SQUAD

Goalkeepers:
Thomas N'Kono, Antoine Bell

Midfield:
Theophile Abega, Gregoire M'Bida, Jean Daniel Eboue, Jean Pierre Tokoto, Joseph Kamga

Forwards:
Roger Milla, Paul Bahoken, Jacques N'Guea, Jean Manga

Onguene, Simon Echoubase, Alain Eyobo, Eugene Ekoule, Martin Maya

Defenders:

Edmond Enoka, Rene Njeya, Francois N'Doumbe Lea, Effrem M'Bom, Gilbert Akono, Ibrahim Aoudou, Michel Kaham, Gregoire Mundeleba, Jacques Kingue

Manager:

Rudi Gutendorf (West Germany). Age 55. Appointed 1982. Was Australia's national coach

WEST GERMANY Group 2, seeded

Formed: 1900
Joined FIFA: 1904–1945; 1950
Clubs: 17,549
Teams: 115,145
Players: 3,611,431
Referees: 40,000
Div. 1 clubs: 18
Season: Aug–June
Colours: White shirts, black shorts, white stockings
Change: Green shirts, white shorts, white stockings

Tenth appearance in World Cup finals. Winners: 1954, 1974; Runners-up: 1966; Third: 1934, 1970; Fourth: 1958

1982 qualifying results:

Bulgaria (A) 3-1, (H) 4-0; Albania (A) 2-0, (H) 8-0; Austria (H) 2-0, (A) 3-1; Finland (A) 4-0, (H) 7-1

Goalscorers:

Rummenigge 9, Fischer 7, Kaltz 5, Breitner 3, Littbarski 3, Schuster 2, Briegel, Dremmler, Magath, own goal

Other 1981 results:

Argentina (N) 1-2; Brazil (N) 1-4 (both Copa de Oro, Uruguay); Brazil (H) 1-2; Poland (A) 2-0

1982:

Portugal (H) 3-1

Strengths:

Tactically flexible, talent in depth, confident and free-scoring

Weakness:
Vulnerable to outside pressures, leading to over-cautious approach

STARS TO WATCH

Karl-Heinz Rummenigge (Bayern Munich). Skill, speed and scoring flair. European F of Y twice. Neat footwork catches opponents off balance. Age 26. 50 caps

Paul Breitner (Bayern Munich). Forceful midfield player, once a full-back. Penalty taker. Reads the game cleverly; uplifting presence. Age 30. 37 caps

Manny Kaltz (Hamburg). Unhappy as sweeper in 1978; formidable right-back with overlapping prowess and firm, accurate finish in the modern mould. Age 29. 56 caps

SQUAD

Goalkeepers:
Harald Schumacher, Bernard Franke, Eike Immel
Defenders:
Karl-Heinz Forster, Bernd Forster, Gerd Strack, Wilfried Hannes, Hans Peter Briegel, Manny Kaltz, Bernd Schuster, Bernd Dietz

Midfield:
Wolfgang Dremmler, Rainer Bonhof, Felix Magath, Paul Breitner, Ulrich Stielike, Hansi Muller, Karl Allgower, Lothar Matthaus, Karl-Heinze Geils

Forwards:
Horst Hrubesch, Karl-Heinz Rummenigge, Ronald Borchers, Klaus Allofs, Thomas Allofs, Klaus Fischer, Pierre Littbarski, Frank Mill, Uwe Reinders

Manager:
Jupp Derwall (West Germany). Age 55. Appointed 1978. Ex-assistant

ALGERIA Group 2
Formed: 1962
Joined FIFA: 1964
Clubs: 780
Teams: 2,607

Players: 58,567
Referees: 1,098
Div. 1 clubs: 16
Season: Sept–June
Colours: Green shirts, white shorts, red stockings
Change: All white

First appearance in World Cup finals

1982 qualifying results:
Sierra Leone (A) 2-2, (H) 3-1; Sudan (H) 2-0, (A) 1-1; Niger (H) 4-0, (A) 0-1; Nigeria (A) 2-0, (H) 2-1

Goalscorers:
Belloumi 3, Bensaoula 3, Fergani 3, Madjer 2, Chebel, Gamouh, Kourichi, Menad, Zidane

Other 1981 results:
Mali (A) 0-3; Iran (H) 1-0; Upper Volta (H) 7-0

1982:
Tunisia (A) 1-0

Strengths:
Midfield, defence; capable of varying tactics

Weakness:
Attack; lack of physical presence

STARS TO WATCH

Lakhdar Belloumi (Mascara). Creative midfield player, useful marksman with either foot. Aged 22. Current African F of Y. More than 30 appearances

Ali Fergani (Tizi-Ouzou). A pillar of club and country in the middle of the field. Fine control and distribution. Age 29. 43 appearances

Mustapha Dahleb (Paris St Germain, France). Noted for his neat left foot touches in midfield and close control. Age 30. Has made 13 appearances

SQUAD

Goalkeepers:
Mehdi Cerbah, Lyacine Bentaala, Mourad Amara

Defenders:
Mahmoud Guendouz, Bouzid Mahyouz, Abdelkader Horr, Rabah Djennadi, Salah Larbes, Mustapha Kouici, Faouzi Mansouri, Norredine Kourichi, Abdel Djaadaoui

Midfield:
Said Kaci, Ali Fergani, Fethi Chebel, Hocine Yahi, Mustapha Dahleb, Lakhdar Belloumi, Mohamed Hamini

Forwards:
Salah Assad, Djamel Zidane, Rabah Gamouh, Rabah Madjer, Tadj Bensaoula

Manager:
Evgeny Rogov (USSR). Age 52. Appointed 1981. Former Algerian club manager

CHILE Group 2
Formed: 1895
Joined FIFA: 1912
Clubs: 5,615
Teams: 13,620
Players: 324,422
Referees: 5,520
Div. 1 clubs: 16
Season: Apr–Dec
Colours: Red shirts, blue shorts, white stockings
Change: All white

Sixth appearance in World Cup finals. Third: 1962

1982 qualifying results:
Ecuador (A) 0-0, (H) 2-0; Paraguay (A) 1-0, (H) 3-0

Goalscorers:
Caszely 2, Yanez 2, Neira, Rivas

Other 1981 results:
Colombia (H) 1-0; Brazil (A) 1-2; Colombia (A) 2-1; Peru (H) 3-0; Uruguay (H) 1-2; Spain (H) 1-1; Uruguay (A) 0-0; Peru (A) 2-1; Brazil (H) 0-0

Strengths:
Well coached; especially accomplished in defence; play within limitations

Weakness:
Suspect temperament; minimal European experience

STARS TO WATCH

Patricio Yanez (San Luis). Right-side attacker with eye-catching ability to penetrate defences. Fine skills in possession. Age 21. Recovered recently from illness

Carlos Caszely (Colo Colo). Experienced centre-forward ex-winger, veteran of 1974 World Cup side. Top scorer with club champions. Has also played in Spain. Quick, accurate. Age 31

Elias Figueroa (Colo Colo). Central defensive organiser. 3 times South American F of Y. Has played in Uruguay, Brazil and USA. Local hero, model player. Age 35

SQUAD

Goalkeepers:
Oscar Wirth, Mario Osben

Defenders:
Mario Soto, Elias Figueroa, Rene Valenzuela, Osvaldo Vargas, Santiago Gatica, Mario Galindo, Lizardo Garrido, Enzo Escobar

Midfield:
Manuel Rojas, Eduardo Bonvallet, Miguel Neira, Rodolfo Dubo, Carlos Rivas, Orlando Mondaca

Forwards:
Rodrigo Santander, Patricio Yanez, Carlos Caszely, Jose Alvarez, Gustavo Moscoso, Leonardo Veliz, Oscar Herrera

Manager:
Oscar Luis Santibanez (Chile). Age 44. Appointed 1978. Former club coach

AUSTRIA Group 2

Formed: 1904
Joined FIFA: 1905
Clubs: 2,041
Teams: 6,466
Players: 255,125
Referees: 1,935
Div. 1 clubs: 10

Season: Aug–Dec; Feb–June
Colours: White shirts, black shorts, black stockings
Change: Red shirts, white shorts, red stockings

Fifth appearance in World Cup finals. Third: 1954; Fourth: 1934

1982 qualifying results:
Finland (A) 2-0, (H) 5-1; Albania (H) 5-0, (A) 1-0; West Germany (A) 0-2, (H) 1-3; Bulgaria (H) 2-0, (A) 0-0

Goalscorers:
Welzl 4, Krankl 3, Schachner 3, Jara 2, Prohaska 2, Jurtin, Pezzey

Other 1981 results:
Spain (H) 0-0; Israel (A) 0-1

Strengths:
Key players with foreign teams have widened individual experience

Weakness:
Failure of domestic clubs to achieve international success

STARS TO WATCH

Herbert Prohaska (Inter-Milan, Italy). Midfield player who has added composure and confidence to his scheming and shooting. Age 26. Formerly FK Austria. 55 caps

Bruno Pezzey (Eintracht Frankfurt, West Germany). Commanding sweeper, organiser in defence, prompter in attack. Age 27. Once with Innsbruck. 52 caps

Walter Schachner (Cesena, Italy). Striker either on wings or in the centre. Scores mostly inside penalty area. 34 goals 1979–80 FK Austria. Age 25. 28 caps

SQUAD

Goalkeepers:
Herbert Feurer, Friedl Koncilia, Johan Pregesbauer

Defenders:
Johan Dihanic, Bernd Krauss, Heribert Weber, Erich Hintermayer, Bruno Pezzey, Mario Zuenelli, Dieter Mirnegg

Midfield:
Roland Hattenberger, Herbert Prohaska, Kurt Jara, Felix

Gasselich, Willy Kreuz, Reinhard Hintermayer, Ernst Baumeister, Helmut Wartinger

Forwards:

Walter Schachner, Hans Krankl, Christian Keglevits, Gernot Jurtin, Kurt Welzl, Max Hagmayer

Manager:

Georg Schmidt (Austria). Age 54. Appointed 1982. Former assistant coach

ARGENTINA Group 3, seeded

Formed: 1893
Joined FIFA: 1912
Clubs: 2,713
Teams: 14,728
Players: 299,895
Referees: 3,272
Div. 1 clubs: 18
Season: March–Dec
Colours: Light blue and white striped shirts, black shorts, white stockings
Change: All blue

Eighth appearance in World Cup finals. Winners: 1978; Runners-up: 1930

Qualified as holders

1981 results:

Brazil (N) 1-1; West Germany (N) 2-1 (both Copa de Oro, Uruguay); Poland (H) 1-2; Czechoslovakia (H) 1-1

Strengths:

Perfected one-touch passing with accuracy and at speed

Weakness:

Lack competitive matches and inspiration of local support from 1978

STARS TO WATCH

Daniel Passarella (River Plate). 72 caps. Central defender excelling at tackling and interceptions. Good eye for attacking options. Inspirational captain 1978. Age 28

Diego Maradona (Boca Juniors). Attacking midfield player of exceptional ability. Has vision, supreme control and confidence. Ace marksman. 29 caps. Age 21. Ex-South American F of Y

Osvaldo Ardiles (Tottenham Hotspur, England). Perpetual motion in midfield; regularly clocks 100 'play' contacts in covering 8,000 metres a match. Age 29. 62 caps

SQUAD

Goalkeepers:
Ubaldo Fillol, Hector Baley, Nery Pumpido

Defenders:
Jorge Olguin, Julio Olarticoechea, Luis Galvan, Alberto Tarantini, Daniel Passarella, Enzo Trossero, Jose Van Tuyne

Midfield:
Americo Gallego, Osvaldo Ardiles, Juan Alberto Barbas, Patricio Hernandez, Victor Heredia, Daniel Valencia

Forwards:
Daniel Bertoni, Ramon Diaz, Enzo Ferrero, Diego Maradona, Daniel Brailovsky, Mario Kempes, Leopoldo Luque, Gabriel Calderon

Manager:
Cesar Luis Menotti (Argentina). Age 43. Appointed 1974. Former player

BELGIUM Group 3

Formed: 1895
Joined FIFA: 1904
Clubs: 3,275
Teams: 14,400
Players: 279,420
Referees: 5,546
Div. 1 clubs: 18
Season: July–June
Colours: All white.
Change: Red shirts, black shorts, yellow stockings

Sixth appearance in World Cup finals

1982 qualifying results:
Eire (A) 1-1, (H) 1-0; Netherlands (H) 1-0, (A) 0-3; Cyprus (A) 2-0, (H) 3-2; France (A) 2-3, (H) 2-0

Goalscorers:
Van den Bergh 5, Ceulemans 4, Cluytens, Czerniatynski, Plessers

Other 1981 results:
Spain (A) 0-2

Strengths: Rigorously competent defence; flowing counter-attacks from midfield

Weakness:
Inconsistency; over-reliance on key players

STARS TO WATCH

Wilfried Van Moer (Beveren). Midfield player of class and vision; influential on team's performance. Age 37. Inspired 1980 European Championship runners-up. 51 caps

Jan Ceulemans (FC Bruges). Good control and finish up front; well drilled in chasing half chances on the break. Age 24. Impressed in European Championship. 26 caps

Erwin Van den Bergh (Lierse). Tall, well built striker with surprising finesse and mobility. 39 League goals 1979–80. Age 23. Usual penalty taker. 15 caps

SQUAD

Goalkeepers:
Jean Marie Pfaff, Michel Preud'homme, Jacques Munaron

Defenders:
Marc Baecke, Michel Renquin, Luc Millecamps, Michel De Wolf, Walter Meeuws, Eric Gerets, Gerard Plessers

Midfield:
Wilfried Van Moer, Marc Millecamps, Rene Vandereycken, Ludo Coeck, Juan Lozano, Frankie Vercauteren, Raymond Mommens, Rene Verheyen, Guy Dardenne

Forwards:
Jan Ceulemans, Erwin Van den Bergh, Alex Czerniatynski, Albert Cluytens, Willy Geurts, Francois Van der Elst

Manager:
Guy Thys (Belgium). Age 60. Appointed 1977. Former international

HUNGARY Group 3

Formed: 1901
Joined FIFA: 1907
Clubs: 2,440
Teams: 5,326
Players: 138,461
Referees: 4,660
Div. 1 clubs: 18
Season: Sept–Dec; March–June
Colours: Red shirts, white shorts, green stockings
Change: All white

Eighth appearance in World Cup finals. Runners-up: 1938, 1954

1982 qualifying results:
Switzerland (A) 2-2, (H) 3-0; Rumania (H) 1-0, (A) 0-0; Norway (A) 2-1, (H) 4-1; England (H) 1-3, (A) 0-1

Goalscorers:
Kiss 4, Fazekas 3, Balint 2, Nyilasi 2, Garaba, Muller

Other 1981 results:
Spain (A) 3-0; Kuwait (H) 1-0

1982:
New Zealand (A) 2-1; New Zealand (A) 2-1

Strengths:
Tradition of encouraging free-flowing build-up

Weakness:
Suspect in penetrating ideas; rhythm often easily upset

STARS TO WATCH

Tibor Nyilasi (Ferencvaros). Tall, adventurous and elegantly arrogant. Excels at the wall-pass and shielding the ball. Fine marksman. Age 26. 47 caps

Andras Torocsik (Ujpest Dozsa). Fiery, opportunist improviser in attack. Fine close control, good finish. Apathetic to training. Age 25. 31 caps

Laszlo Kiss (Vasas Budapest). Usually plays on the left in attack. Drawn magnet-like to goal, but inclined to overdo individualism. Firm shooting ability. Age 25. 20 caps

SQUAD

Goalkeepers:

Ferenc Meszaros, Bela Katzirz, Laszlo Kakas

Defenders:

Gyozo Martos, Laszlo Balint, Gabor Szanto, Imre Garaba, Attila Kerekes, Tibor Rab, Jozsef Toth, Jozset Varga

Midfield:

Sandor Muller, Andras Komjati, Karoly Csapo, Sandor Sallai, Miklos Moldvan, Tibor Nyilasi, Sandor Zombori

Forwards:

Laszlo Fazekas, Andras Torocsik, Laszlo Kiss, Bela Bodonyi, Ignac Izso, Gyorgy Kerekes, Laszlo Fekete

Manager:

Kalman Meszoly (Hungary). Age 41. Appointed 1980. Former international

EL SALVADOR Group 3

Formed: 1935
Joined FIFA: 1938
Clubs: 782
Teams: 620
Players: 16,396
Referees: 463
Div. 1 clubs: 12
Season: Jan–Nov
Colours: All blue
Change: All white

Second appearance in World Cup finals

1982 qualifying results:

Panama (A) 3-1, (H) 4-1; Costa Rica (H) 2-0*, (A) 0-0; Guatemala (A) 0-0, (H) 1-0; Honduras (H) 2-1, (A) 0-2, (A) 0-0; Canada (A) 0-1; Mexico (A) 1-0; Cuba (A) 0-0; Haiti (A) 1-0

Goalscorers:

Gonzalez 5, Huezo 3, Rivas 2, Fernandez, Guerrero. (*Not played; won 2-0 on forfeit)

Other 1981 results:

Haiti (A) 0-0; Haiti (A) 0-0; Haiti (H) 4-0; Portugal (H) 2-1

1982:

Rumania (H) 2-1

Strengths:

Defence reasonably well organised.

Weakness:

Anaemic attack; domestic crisis worries

STARS TO WATCH

Jose Norberto Huezo (Atletico Marte). Chief organiser and distributor, specialising in accurate defensive-splitting passes. Captain. Age 26. 45 caps

Jorge Gonzalez (Deportivo FAS). Attacking midfield player likened to a Central American Maradona. Persistent, strong shot. Nickname 'Magic'. Age 21. 34 caps

Luis Guevara Mora (Platense). Goalkeeper who will have every opportunity to show his ability. Quick and courageous and a promising prospect. Age 21. 14 caps

SQUAD

Goalkeepers:

Luis Guevara Mora, Eduardo Hernandez, Carlos Rivera

Defenders:

Mario Castillo, Jaime Rodriguez, Ramon Alfredo Fagoaga, Carlos Humberto Recinos, Francisco Salvador Osorto, Jose Francisco Jovel, Miguel Angel Arevaro

Midfield:

Juan Gilberto Quinteros, Mauricio Alberto Alfaro, Jose Norberto Huezo, Jose Luis Rugamas, Miguel Guillermo Gonzalez, Silvio Romeo Aquino, Joaquin Alonso Ventura, Freddy Rivera

Forwards:

Jorge Gonzalez, Francisco Ever Hernandez, Oscar Gustavo Guerrero, Jose Antonio Infantozzi, Jose Miguel Escamilla, Jose Maria Rivas, Mauricio Quintanilla

Manager:

Mauricio 'Pipo' Rodriguez (El Salvador). Age 36. Appointed 1980. Ex-player

ENGLAND Group 4, seeded

Formed: 1863
Joined FIFA:
1905–1920; 1924–1928; 1946
Clubs: 37,715
Teams: 36,904
Players: 1,505,000
Referees: 9,500
Div. 1 clubs: 22
Season: Aug–June
Colours: White shirts, royal blue shorts, white stockings
Change: Red shirts, white shorts, red stockings

Seventh appearance in World Cup finals. Winners: 1966

1982 qualifying results:
Norway (H) 4-0, (A) 1-2; Rumania (A) 1-2, (H) 0-0; Switzerland (H) 2-1, (A) 1-2; Hungary (A) 3-1, (H) 1-0

Goalscorers:
McDermott 3, Mariner 3, Brooking 2, Woodcock 2, Keegan, Robson, own goal

Other 1981 results:
Spain (H) 1-2; Brazil (H) 0-1; Wales (H) 0-0; Scotland (H) 0-1

1982:
N. Ireland (H) 4-0

Strengths: Difficult to score goals against; encouraged to express individualism

Weakness: Failure to sustain authority and poor finishers

STARS TO WATCH

Kevin Keegan (Southampton). Instinctive inspirational captain. Twice European F of Y. Fine balance, low gravity centre. Pace and craft breaks up defences. Age 31. 60 caps

Bryan Robson (Manchester United). Most consistent player in past 18 months. Age 25. Midfield sweeper, tidies up cleverly. Offensive ideas and scoring prowess. 15 caps

Trevor Brooking (West Ham United). Master of the weighted pass, remarkable midfield vision. Highly rated on continent. Unselfish approach. 45 caps. Age 33

SQUAD

Goalkeepers:

Ray Clemence, Peter Shilton, Joe Corrigan

Defenders:

Viv Anderson, Kenny Sansom, Phil Thompson, Dave Watson, Phil Neal, Mick Mills, Russell Osman, Alvin Martin, Steve Foster

Midfield:

Bryan Robson, Ray Wilkins, Trevor Brooking, Glenn Hoddle, Terry McDermott, Eric Gates, Graham Rix

Forwards:

Paul Mariner, Tony Woodcock, Steve Coppell, Trevor Francis, Kevin Keegan, Tony Morley, Cyrille Regis, Peter Withe

Manager:

Ron Greenwood (England). Age 61. Appointed 1977. Former West Ham manager

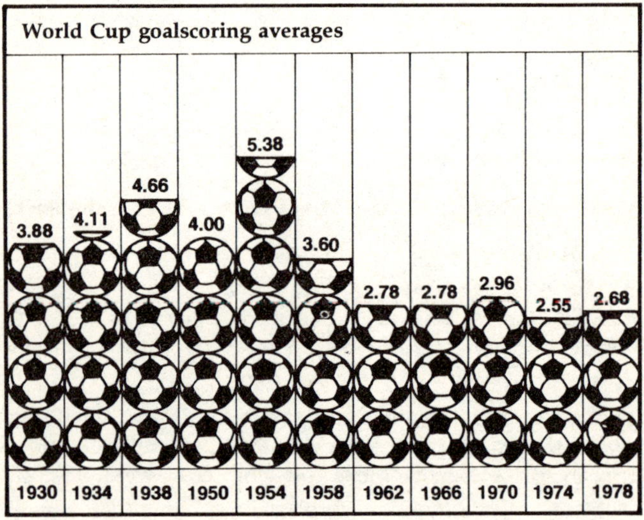

FRANCE Group 4

Formed: 1919
Joined FIFA: 1904
Clubs: 18,285
Teams: 52,000
Players: 1,194,189
Referees: 14,907
Div. 1 clubs: 20
Season: July–Dec; Jan–June
Colours: Blue shirts, white shorts, red stockings
Change: White shirts, blue shorts, red stockings

Eighth appearance in World Cup finals. Third: 1958

1982 qualifying results:
Cyprus (A) 7-0, (H) 4-0; Eire (H) 2-0, (A) 2-3; Belgium (H) 3-2, (A) 0-2; Netherlands (A) 0-1, (H) 2-0

Goalscorers:
Platini 5, Lacombe 3, Six 3, Larios 2, Soler 2, Zimako 2, Bellone, Rocheteau, Genghini

Other 1981 results:
Spain (A) 0-1; Brazil (H) 1-3

1982:
Italy (H) 2-0

Strengths:
Purposeful, open attractive style of pressurising opponents

Weakness: Erratic and prone to elementary errors

STARS TO WATCH

Michel Platini (St. Etienne). Mercurial midfield master and captain. Talented fulcrum of French ambitions. Artistic marksman. Age 26. 33 caps. Free-kick ace

Marius Tresor (Bordeaux). Industrious sweeper who has overcome succession of injuries. Covers and tackles with efficiency; authoritative figure. Age 32. 50 caps

Dominique Rocheteau (Paris St Germain). Freed from restrictive right side role in attack; wanders cleverly. Skilful, inventive forward with fine control. Age 27. 23 caps

SQUAD

Goalkeepers:

Jean Castaneda, Dominique Baratelli, Pierrick Hiard

Defenders:

Dominique Bathenay, Patrick Battiston, Philippe Mahut, Max Bossis, Gerard Janvion, Christian Lopez, Marius Tresor, Manuel Amoros

Midfield:

Jean-Francois Larios, Didier Christophe, Michel Platini, Jean Tigana, Daniel Bravo, Alain Giresse, Bernard Ghenghini, Alain Moizan

Forwards:

Didier Six, Jacques Zimako, Bernard Lacombe, Gerard Soler, Bruno Bellone, Alain Couriol, Dominique Rocheteau

Manager:

Michel Hidalgo (France). Age 49. Appointed 1975. Former international

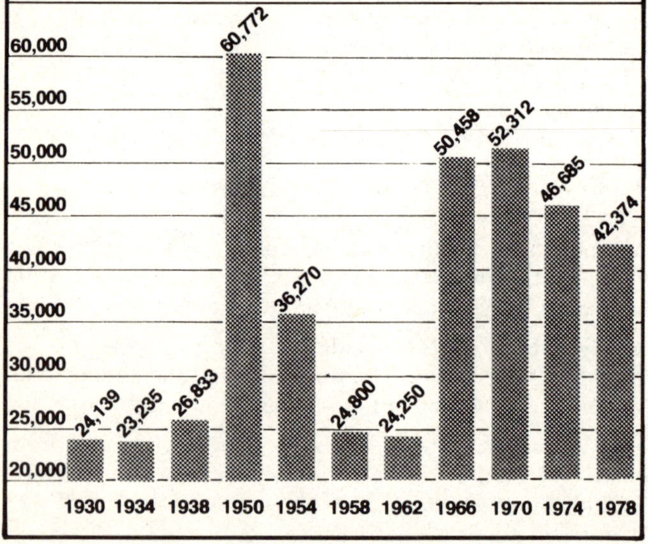

World Cup attendance averages

CZECHOSLOVAKIA Group 4

Formed: 1901
Joined FIFA: 1906
Clubs: 6,776
Teams: 26,847
Players: 352,227
Referees: 6,550
Div. 1 clubs: 16
Season: Aug–Nov; Feb–June
Colours: Red shirts, white shorts, blue stockings
Change: All white

Seventh appearance in World Cup finals. Runners-up: 1934, 1962

1982 qualifying results:
Wales (A) 0-1, (H) 2-0; Turkey (H) 2-0, (A) 3-0; Iceland (H) 6-1, (A) 1-1; USSR (A) 0-2, (H) 1-1

Goalscorers:
Kozak 4, Nehoda 3, Janecka 2, Vizek 2, Licka, Panenka, Voyacek, own goal

Other 1981 results:
Bolivia (A) 1-2; Bolivia (A) 5-2; Peru (A) 3-1; Switzerland (H) 0-1; Eire (A) 1-3; Argentina (A) 1-1

Strengths:
Precise, close passing game; well organised

Weakness:
Stress on individual skill against tight-marking defences

STARS TO WATCH

Frantisek Jakubec (Bohemians). Right-back who favours the modern overlapping approach. Quick, accurate and a marksman. Age 26. 6 caps. Discovered by Tomas Pospichal

Zdenek Nehoda (Dukla Prague). Poacher of goals with fine record 140 in League; 31 in 82 internationals. Plays slightly deeper these days. Age 29

Antonin Panenka (Rapid Vienna, Austria). Gifted but inconsistent midfield player. Age 33. Schemer excelling at dead ball situations. 56 appearances

SQUAD

Goalkeepers:
Zdenek Hruska, Stanislav Seman, Jaroslav Netolicka

Defenders:
Frantisek Jakubec, Rostislav Vojacek, Premysl Bicovsky, Jozef Barmos, Libor Radimec, Jan Fiala, Ladislav Jurkemik, Ludek Macela

Midfield:
Jan Kozak, Antonin Panenka, Jan Berger, Frantisek Stambachr, Petr Nemec, Zdenek Srajner, Werner Licka

Forwards:
Tomas Kriz, Ladislav Vizek, Marian Masny, Zdenek Nehoda, Petr Janecka, Lubos Pokluda, Zdenek Valek

Manager:
Dr. Jozef Venglos (Czechoslovakia). Age 46. Appointed 1978. Former assistant

KUWAIT Group 4

Formed: 1952
Joined FIFA: 1962
Clubs: 14 (Div. 1)
Teams: 28
Players: 1,638
Referees: 51
Season: Oct–May
Colours: Blue shirts, white shorts, blue stockings
Change: Red shirts, white shorts, red stockings

First appearance in World Cup finals

1982 qualifying results:
Thailand (H) 6-0; Malaysia (H) 4-0; South Korea (H) 2-0; New Zealand (A) 2-1, (H) 2-2; China (A) 0-3, (H) 1-0; Saudi Arabia (A) 1-0, (H) 2-0

Goalscorers:
Anbari 5, Dakheel 4, Yacoub 3, Jomah 2, Kameel 2, Ghanem 2, Hashash, Karam

Other 1981 results:
Hungary (A) 0-1

Strengths: Well drilled, dedicated squad on Brazilian style

Weakness: Prone to defensive error and lack of physical presence

STARS TO WATCH

Abdul Aziz Al Anbari (Kuwait). The most capped international in the team having made 84 appearances. Skilful left-wing striker. Age 28. Government employee

Faisal Al Dakheel (Al Qadisiya). Forward with a reputation of marksmanship. Employed by Kuwait Airways. Made his international debut 1974. Age 25. 68 caps

Ahmed Al Tarabulsy (Kuwait). Enhanced an already fine reputation in Asia, when he played in the Moscow Olympics in 1980. Goalkeeper. Army Sergeant. Age 34. 55 caps

SQUAD:

Goalkeepers:

Ahmed Al Tarabulsy, Ali Al Sayed, Adam Marjam Adam

Defenders: Sami Al Hashash, Naeem Saad, Mahboud Jomah Mubarak, Waleed Jassem Mubarek, Abdullah Mayouf, Jamal Yacoub, Abdul Nabi, Hamoud Fleitah

Midfield:

Abdullah Baloushi, Mohammed Karam, Ahmad Askar, Ahmed Al Darwish, Mubarak Marzouk, Nasser Al Ghanem, Saad Al Houti

Forwards:

Jassem Yacoub, Fathi Kameel, Faisal Al Dakheel, Abdul Aziz Al Anbari, Yussef Swayed, Saad Shabib

Manager:

Carlos Alberto Parreira (Brazil). Age 39. Appointed 1978. Ex-Brazil assistant coach

---

Leading World Cup goalscorers (final tournament)

Year	Name	Country	Goals
1930	Guillermo Stabile	Argentina	8
1934	Angelo Schiavio	Italy	4
	Oldrich Nejedly	Czechoslovakia	4
	Edmund Conen	Germany	4

1938	Leonidas da Silva	Brazil	8
1950	Ademir	Brazil	7
1954	Sandor Kocsis	Hungary	11
1958	Just Fontaine	France	13
1962	Drazen Jerkovic	Yugoslavia	5
1966	Eusebio	Portugal	9
1970	Gerd Muller	West Germany	10
1974	Grzegorz Lato	Poland	7
1978	Mario Kempes	Argentina	6

SPAIN Group 5, seeded

Formed: 1913
Joined FIFA: 1904
Clubs: 5,578
Teams: 5,578
Players: 202,574
Referees: 5,305
Div. 1 clubs: 18
Season: Sept–June
Colours: Red shirts, blue shorts, black stockings
Change: Blue shirts, blue shorts, black stockings

Sixth appearance in World Cup finals. Fourth: 1950

Qualified as hosts

1981 results:
France (H) 1-0; England (A) 2-1; Hungary (H) 0-3; Portugal (A) 0-2; Mexico (A) 1-2; Mexico (A) 3-1; Venezuela (A) 2-0; Colombia (A) 1-1; Chile (A) 1-1; Brazil (A) 0-1; Austria (A) 0-0; Luxembourg (H) 3-0; Poland (A) 3-2; Belgium (H) 2-0

1982:
Scotland (H) 3-0

Strengths:
Home advantage, local backing; useful defence, midfield

Weakness: Over-cautious; forward problems

STARS TO WATCH
Jesus Zamora (Real Sociedad). A hybrid: organiser, inspiration and goalscorer from midfield berth. Excels at finding openings. Cool, clever skills. Age 26. 25 caps

Luis Arconada (Real Sociedad). Athletic goalkeeper; confident, often spectacular; eye-catching appeal and expert at smothering solo attacks. Age 27. 37 caps

Jose Camacho (Real Madrid). Tough tackling but adroit defender who can operate as a full-back or a defensive midfield marker. Recovered from serious injury. Age 26. 27 caps

SQUAD

Goalkeepers:

Luis Arconada, Miguel Angel, Jose Manuel Sampere

Defenders:

Ricardo Panela Arias, Juan Jose Estella, Antonio Maceda, Genaro Celayeta, Miguel Tendillo, Jose Ramon Alesanco, Jose Camacho, Rafael Gordillo, Manuel Jimenez

Midfield:

Enrique Saura, Victor Munoz, Enrique Ramos Quique, Ricardo Gallego, Miguel Alonso, Jesus Zamora, Jose Vicente, Jose Cano Canito

Forwards:

Jesus Satrustegui, Roberto Lopez Ufarte, Vigo Esteban, Carlos Santillana, Juanito, Alonso Marcos, Quini, Enrique Moran

Manager:

Jose Santamaria (Uruguay, naturalised Spain). Age 52. Appointed 1980. Ex-club coach

---

Best individual goalscoring in one World Cup Match
(final tournament). Each player scored 4 goals.

Name	For		Against
Gustav Wetterstroem	Sweden	v	Cuba 1938
Leonidas da Silva	Brazil	v	Poland 1938
Ernest Willimowski	Poland	v	Brazil 1938
Ademir	Brazil	v	Sweden 1950
Juan Schiaffino	Uruguay	v	Bolivia 1950
Sandor Kocsis	Hungary	v	West Germany 1954
Just Fontaine	France	v	West Germany 1958
Eusebio	Portugal	v	North Korea 1966

HONDURAS Group 5

Formed: 1951
Joined FIFA: 1951
Clubs: 452
Teams: 450
Players: 11,550
Referees: 423
Div. 1 clubs: 12
Season: Feb–Dec
Colours: Blue shirts, white shorts, blue stockings
Change: All white

First appearance in World Cup finals

1982 qualifying results:
Panama (A) 2-0, (H) 5-0; Costa Rica (A) 3-2, (H) 1-1; Guatemala (H) 0-0, (A) 1-0; El Salvador (A) 1-2, (H) 2-0, (H) 0-0; Haiti (H) 4-0; Cuba (H) 2-0; Canada (H) 2-1; Mexico (H) 0-0

Goalscorers:
Bailey 6, Figueroa 6, Bernardez 5, Buezo 2, Costly J., Caballero, Urquia, Velazquez

1982:
Rumania (H) 0-0

Strengths:
Useful knowledge from two successive Spanish pre-season tournaments

Weakness:
Squandering chances – and will have far fewer

STARS TO WATCH

Ramon Maradiaga (Motagua). Tight, defensive marker in midfield and useful inspiration all round. Nickname 'El Primitivo'. Tenacious and energetic with attacking ideas. Age 26

Jimmy Bailey (Marathon). Product of fine Honduras youth team in FIFA–Coca Cola Cup. Reliable marksman in early qualifying games. Suffered knee injury. Age 26

Roberto Figueroa (Deportivo Vida). Tall, fast striker with constructive and finishing ability in the penalty area. Nicknamed 'Macho'. Age 22

SQUAD

Goalkeepers:

Julio Arzu, Jimmy Steward, Belarmino Rivera, Oscar Benegas

Defenders:

Efrain Gutierrez, Domingo Drummond, Hernan Garcia, Fernando Bulnes, Anthony Costly, Hector Zelaya, Jaime Villegas, Luis Cruz

Midfield:

Ramon Maradiaga, Javier Toledo, David Bueso, Juan Murillo

Forwards:

Jimmy Bailey, Salvador Bernardez, Tony Laing, Jorge Urquia, Roberto Figueroa, Orlando Caballero, Junior Costly

Manager:

Jose de la Paz Herrera 'Chelato' Ucles (Honduras). Age 39. Appointed 1979. Ex-coach in Argentina

YUGOSLAVIA Group 5

Formed: 1919
Joined FIFA: 1919
Clubs: 4,289
Teams: 4,289
Players: 172,225
Referees: 6,541
Div. 1 clubs: 18
Season: Aug–Dec; March–June
Colours: Blue shirts, white shorts, red stockings
Change: All white

Seventh appearance in World Cup finals. Semi-finalists: 1930; Fourth: 1962

1982 qualifying results:
Luxembourg (A) 5-0, (H) 5-0; Denmark (H) 2-1, (A) 2-1; Italy (A) 0-2, (H) 1-1; Greece (H) 5-1, (A) 2-1

Goalscorers:
Zlatko Vujovic 7, Halihodzic 3, Pantelic 2, Surjak 2, Petrovic 2,Buljan, Jerkovic, Pasic, Slijivio, Susic, Zoran Vujovic

Other 1981 results: Bulgaria (H) 2-1

Strengths: Capable of imaginative, attacking ideas

Weakness:
Often frustrated by ultra defensive opponents

STARS TO WATCH

Zlatko Vujovic (Hajduk Split). One of twins in the squad. Forward or midfield player. Quick, alert; record as marksman but unselfish. Scored Yugoslavia's 150th WC goal. Age 23. 16 caps

Vladimir Petrovic (Red Star Belgrade). Cultured midfield player with high work rate. Blossomed as teenage left-winger. Fine dead ball artist. Age 26. 30 caps

Ivica Surjak (Paris St Germain, France). Versatile left side midfield player or attacking defender. Age 29. 51 caps. Captains by dedicated example

SQUAD

Goalkeepers:
Dragan Pantelic, Ratko Svilar, Aleksander Stojanovic

Defenders:
Zlatko Krmpotic, Zoran Vujovic, Milos Hrstic, Velimir Zajec, Nenad Stojkovic, Ivan Buljan, Nikola Jovanovic

Midfield:
Ivan Gudelj, Edhem Slijvo, Ivan Jerolimov, Jurica Jerkovic, Vladimir Petrovic, Zvonko Zivkovic, Zlatko Vujovic

Forwards:
Milos Sestic, Blaz Sliskovic, Safet Susic, Vahid Halilhodzic, Pedrag Pasic, Mitar Mrkela, Ivica Surjak

Manager:
Miljan Miljanic (Yugoslavia). Age 51. Appointed 1978. Former Real Madrid manager

NORTHERN IRELAND Group 5

Formed: 1880
Joined FIFA:
1911–1920; 1924–1928; 1946
Clubs: 740
Teams: 875
Players: 17,685
Referees: 352
Div. 1 clubs: 12
Season: Aug–May
Colours: Green shirts, white shorts, green stockings
Change: White shirts, green shorts, green stockings

Second appearance in World Cup finals

1982 qualifying results:
Israel (A) 0-0, (H) 1-0; Sweden (H) 3-0, (A) 0-1; Portugal (A) 0-1, (H) 1-0; Scotland (A) 1-1, (H) 0-0
Goalscorers:
Armstrong 2, Brotherston, Hamilton, McIlroy, Nicholl J.

Other 1981 results:
Scotland (A) 0-2

1982:
England (A) 0-4

Strengths:
Harmony of close-knit club-like spirit, playing above club standard

Weakness:
Lack sufficient players with regular First Division experience

STARS TO WATCH

Pat Jennings (Arsenal). 90th cap v England in February. Vastly experienced goalkeeper; large, safe hands, expert at cutting out angles. Aged 36

Gerry Armstrong (Watford). Strong running centre-forward who takes on defences from any part of the attack. Has also achieved some vital goals. 35 caps. Age 27

Martin O'Neill (Norwich City). Began his career as a winger. Now moved to midfield and has good control and distribution in attack. Captain. 42 caps. Age 30

SQUAD

Goalkeepers:
Pat Jennings, Jim Platt

Defenders
Jimmy Nicholl, Chris Nicholl, John O'Neill, Mal Donaghy, Sammy Nelson, Gerry McElhinney, Pat Rice

Midfield:
Tommy Cassidy, David McCreery, Sammy McIlroy, Martin O'Neill

Forwards:
Noel Brotherston, Gerry Armstrong, Billy Hamilton, Trevor Anderson, Gerry Mullan, Tom Finney, Terry Cochrane, Derek Spence, Tom Sloan

Manager:
Billy Bingham (Northern Ireland). Age 50. Appointed 1980 (second time). Ex-international

BRAZIL Group 6, seeded

Formed: 1914
Joined FIFA: 1923
Clubs: 5,436
Teams: 18,369
Players: 112,755
Referees: 1,266
Div. 1 clubs: None (National championship; State leagues)
Season: Aug–Dec; Jan–June
Colours: Yellow shirts, blue shorts, white stockings
Change: Blue shirts, white shorts, white stockings

Twelfth appearance in World Cup finals: Winners: 1958, 1962, 1970; Runners-up: 1950; Third: 1938, 1978; Fourth: 1974

1982 qualifying results:
Venezuela (A) 1-0, (H) 5-0; Bolivia (A) 2-1, (H) 3-1

Goalscorers:
Zico 5, Socrates 2, Tita 2, Junior, Reinaldo

Other 1981 results:

Argentina (N) 1-1; West Germany (N) 4-1; Uruguay (A) 1-2 (all Copa de Oro, Uruguay); Colombia (A) 1-1; Ecuador (A) 6-0; Chile (H) 2-1; England (A) 1-0; France (A) 3-1; West Germany (A) 2-1; Spain (H) 1-0; Chile (A) 0-0; League of Ireland (H) 6-0; Bulgaria (H) 3-0

1982:

East Germany (H) 3-1

Strengths:

High technical quality; instinctive improvisation

Weakness:

Lack orthodox spearhead; occasional lapses of temperament

STARS TO WATCH

Junior (Flamengo). Free-flowing full-back converted from midfield by the late Claudio Coutinho. Attacking defender in modern sense. Age 27. 32 caps

Zico (Flamengo). South American F of Y. Quick, unselfish with fine control. More than 500 goals in career. Free-kick specialist. Aged 29. 67 caps, 48 goals

Socrates (Corinthians). Nonchalant, unassuming deep-lying centre-forward and attack organiser. Also Doctor of Medicine. Age 27. Penalty taker. 31 caps

SQUAD

Goalkeepers:

Valdir Peres, Paulo Sergio, Carlos

Defenders:

Leandro, Edevaldo, Junior, Luisinho, Perivaldo, Pedrinho, Juninho, Edinho

Midfield:

Cerezo, Batista, Socrates, Falcao, Zico, Renato

Forwards:

Roberto, Mario Sergio, Paulo Isidoro, Serginho, Ze Sergio, Eder

Manager:

Tele Santana (Brazil). Age 50. Appointed 1980. Former club coach

USSR Group 6

Formed: 1912
Joined FIFA: 1946
Clubs: 50,664
Teams: 164
Players: 4,505,000
Referees: 136,380
Div. 1 clubs: 16
Season: Apr–Nov
Colours: Red shirts, white shorts, red stockings
Change: All white

Fifth appearance in World Cup finals. Fourth: 1966

1982 qualifying results:
Iceland (H) 5-0, (A) 2-1; Wales (A) 0-0, (H) 3-0; Turkey (H) 4-0, (A) 3-0; Czechoslovakia (H) 2-0, (A) 1-1

Goalscorers:
Blokhin 5, Shengelia 4, Andreyev 3, Gavrilov 2, Oganesian 2, Bessonov, Chivadze, Daraselia, Demyanenko

Other 1981 results:
Venezuela (A) 1-1

Strengths:
Defence and successful integration of individualism with team work.

Weakness:
Suspect commitment by some individuals.

STARS TO WATCH

Alexander Chivadze (Dynamo Tbilisi). Marshals with cool authority; play-maker adept at fast breaks from defence. Inspiration, positional skill. Age 27. 15 caps

Ramaz Shengelia (Dynamo Tbilisi). Forceful penetrating attacker, good control. Quick, left side striker and dangerous with neat close in headers. Age 24, 12 caps

Oleg Blokhin (Dynamo Kiev). Former European F of Y. Dangerous raider on the flanks, explosive shot. Skilful, deceptively agile and confident. Age 30. 49 caps

SQUAD

Goalkeepers:

Renat Dasayev, Otari Gabelia, Viktor Chanov

Defenders:

Vagiz Khidiatulin, Tengiz Sulakvelidze, Victor Yanushevsky, Alexander Chivadze, Yuri Susloparov, Sergei Borovski, Sergei Baltacha, Anatoly Demyanenko, Alexander Bubnov

Midfield:

Vitali Daraselia, Andrei Bal, Vladimir Bessonov, Yuri Gavrilov, Leonid Buryak, Sergei Shavlo, David Kipiani

Forwards:

Ramaz Shengelia, Oleg Blokhin, Sergei Andreyev, Khoren Oganesian, Vladimir Gutsaev, Vadim Yevtushenko, Fyodor Cherenkov

Manager:

Konstantin Beskov (USSR). Age 61. Appointed 1979 (second time). Former club manager

SCOTLAND Group 6

Formed: 1873

Joined FIFA:

1910–1920; 1924–1928; 1946

Clubs: 4,074

Teams: 7,100

Players: 109,000

Referees: 1,540

Div. 1 clubs: 10

Season: July–Apr

Colours: Dark blue shirts, white shorts, red stockings

Change: White shirts, blue shorts, white stockings

Fifth appearance in World Cup finals

1982 qualifying results:

Sweden (A) 1-0, (H) 2-0; Portugal (H) 0-0, (A) 1-2; Israel (A) 1-0, (H) 3-1; Northern Ireland (H) 1-1, (A) 0-0

Goalscorers:

Robertson 3, Dalglish, Jordan, Provan, Strachan, Sturrock, Wark

Other 1981 results:
Northern Ireland (H) 2-0; Wales (A) 0-2; England (A) 1-0;

1982:
Spain (A) 0-3

Strengths:
Capable of upsetting better teams; more cleverly coached than previously

Weakness:
Tradition of inconsistency and failure to beat poorer sides

STARS TO WATCH

Kenny Dalglish (Liverpool). Sharp awareness in penalty area; can control, make space and shoot in split-seconds. 82 caps. International form often disappointing. Age 31

Asa Hartford (Manchester C). Captain. Midfield player and former winger who has developed combative skill and industry. 46 caps. Power and discipline, too. Age 31

Alan Hansen (Liverpool). Tall, elegant extra cover defender in the centre, fast developing air of casual control. Tackles and counter-attacks well. Age 26. 11 caps

SQUAD

Goalkeepers:
Alan Rough, Billy Thomson, Jim Leighton

Forwards:
Joe Jordan, John Robertson, Alan Brazil, Andy Gray, Davie Provan, Kenny Dalglish, Steve Archibald, Davie Cooper, Paul Sturrock

Midfield: Gordon Strachan, Archie Gemmill, Roy Aitken, John Wark, Asa Hartford, Graeme Souness

Defenders:
Alan Hansen, Danny McGrain, David Narey, Willie Miller, Ray Stewart, Gordon McQueen, Frank Gray, Alex McLeish

Manager:
Jock Stein (Scotland). Age 59. Appointed 1978. Former Celtic manager

NEW ZEALAND Group 6

Formed: 1891
Joined FIFA: 1948
Clubs: 312
Teams: 3,049
Players: 41,698
Referees: 500
Div. 1 clubs: 12
Season: March–October
Colours: White shirts, black shorts, white stockings
Change: Black shirts, white shorts, white stockings

First appearance in World Cup finals

1982 qualifying results:
Australia (H) 3-3, Fiji (A) 4-0, Taiwan (A) 0-0, Indonesia (A) 2-0, Australia (A) 2-0, Indonesia (H) 5-0, Taiwan (H) 2-0, Fiji (H) 13-0, China (A) 0-0, China (H) 1-0, Kuwait (H) 1-2, Saudi Arabia (H) 2-2, Kuwait (A) 2-2, Saudi Arabia (A) 5-0, China (H) 2-1
Goalscorers:
G. Turner 11, Sumner 8, B. Turner 8, Wooddin 6, Rufer 3, Cole 2, Herbert 2, Elrich, McClure, Mackay, Simonsen

1982 results:
Hungary (H) 1-2, Hungary (H) 1-2

Strengths:
Free-scoring attack especially ruthless against poor opposition

Weakness:
Lack experience against top European and South American teams

STARS TO WATCH

Ricky Herbert (Wellington). Has been on trial with Southampton. Strong all-round defender and useful marksman from set pieces. 19 caps

Steve Sumner (Newcastle, Australia). Captain. Scored 6 goals against Fiji and likes to attack from deep positions. 61 caps

Wynton Rufer (Norwich City). Only 19 and given his first chance two years ago. Fast moving striker who has gained some experience this season with Norwich City reserves. 6 caps

SQUAD

Goalkeepers:
Richard Wilson, Frank Van Hatten, Barry Pickering

Defenders:
Glenn Dods, Ricky Herbert, Bobby Almond, Glen Adam, Dave Bright, Sam Malcolmson, Adrian Elrick, John Hill

Midfield:
Keith Mackay, Steve Sumner, Duncan Cole, Billy McClure, Allan Boath, Peter Simonsen, Kenny Cresswell, Grant Turner

Forwards:
Steve Wooddin, Wynton Rufer, Brian Turner, Clive Campbell

Manager:
John Adshead. 39. Appointed 1979. Formerly club coach

How Will They Play In Spain?

Soccer was once an uncomplicated game of excitement and uncertainty. Then coaches began to devise tactical systems of play. Jack Rollin's diagrams expose an overall negative strategy based on the premise that it is better to play a system that diminishes the probability of the opposition scoring as a result of defensive error than a system that encourages spontaneity and improvisation in attack. In short, coaches have increased the muscle of midfield and defence at the expense of attack.

Taken to its logical conclusion perhaps we will see a 4-3-2-1 formation (the pyramid system?) in Spain this year!

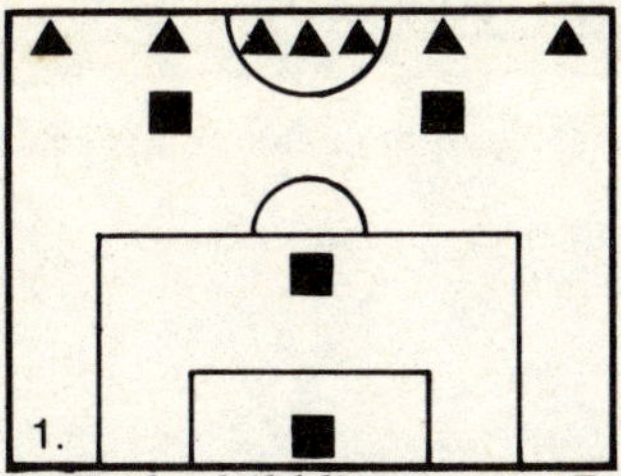

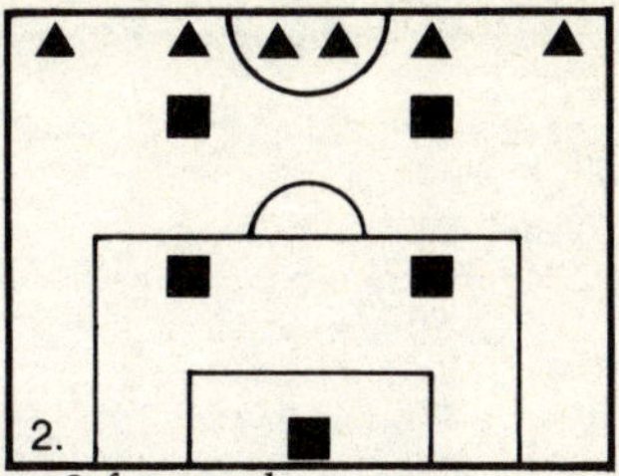

1. Early dribbling game. 7 even 8 forwards.
2. Scotland's withdrawal to stronger midfield in 1870s.

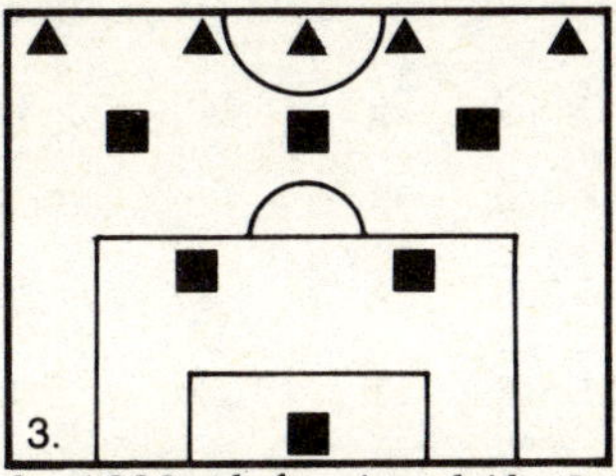

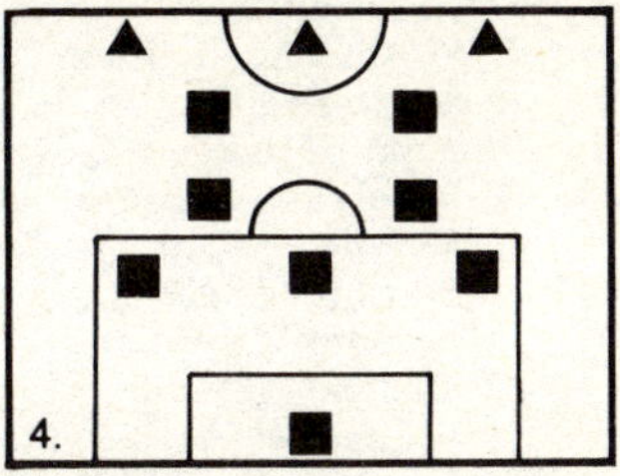

3. 1880s defensive drift. 2-3-5 system.
4. WM formation adds defensive centre-back.

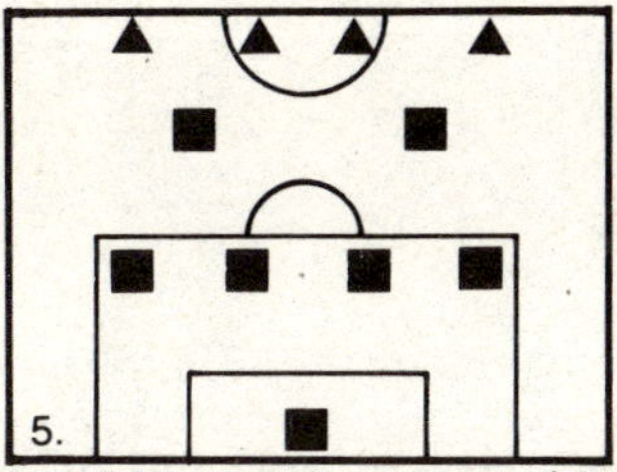

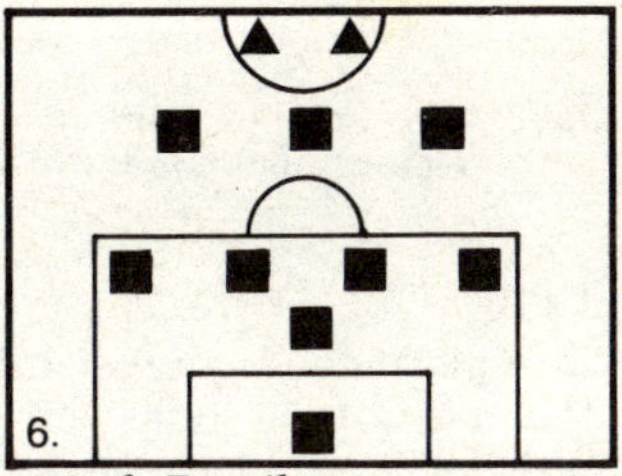

5. 1950s 4-2-4 system of Hungary & Brazil.
6. Italy's ultra-defensive *catenaccio* system of 60s.

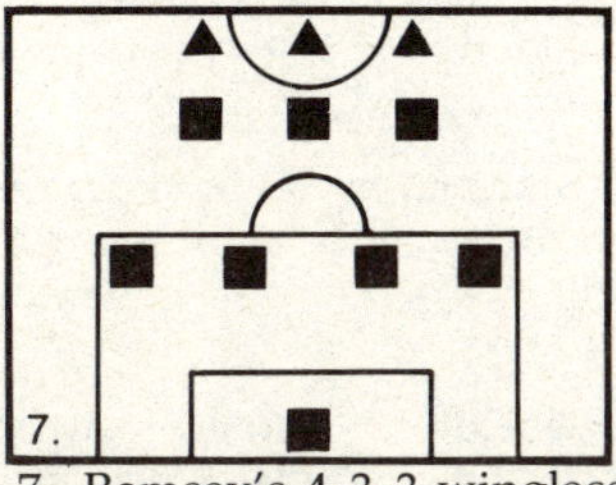

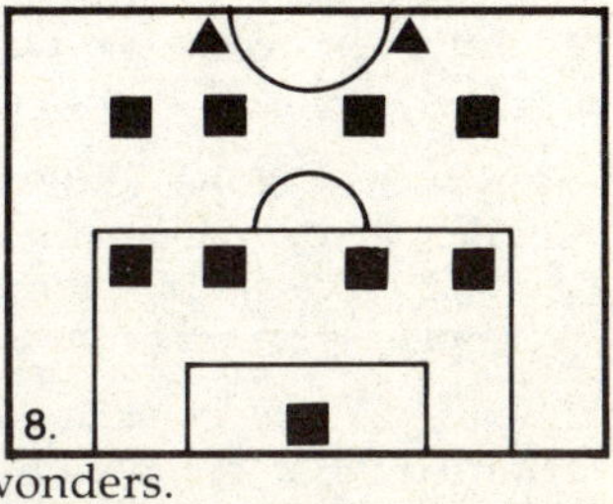

7. Ramsey's 4-3-3 wingless wonders.
8. 4-4-2 heavy midfield system of 70s.

World Cup Facts & Feats, 1930-1978

1930–1978 World Cup winners, managers, attendances and goals

Year	Winners (venue)	Attendances	Games	Goals	Av.
1930	Uruguay (at home) Alberto Supicci	434,500	18	70	3.88
1934	Italy (at home) Vittorio Pozzo	395,000	17	70	4.11
1938	Italy (in France) Vittorio Pozzo	483,000	18	84	4.66
1950	Uruguay (in Brazil) Juan Lopez	1,337,000	22	88	4.00
1954	West Germany (in Switzerland) Sepp Herberger	943,000	26	140	5.38
1958	Brazil (in Sweden) Vicente Feola	868,000	35	126	3.60
1962	Brazil (in Chile) Aymore Moreira	776,000	32	89	2.78
1966	England (at home) Alf Ramsey	1,614,677	32	89	2.78
1970	Brazil (in Mexico) Mario Zagalo	1,673,975	32	95	2.96
1974	West Germany (at home) Helmut Schoen	1,774,022	38	97	2.55
1978	Argentina (at home) Cesar Luis Menotti	1,610,215	38	102	2.68

1930

Europe could only muster 4 teams among the 13 entries for the inaugural series in Uruguay, the prospect of a fortnight's sea journey and an 18-day tournament dissuading others from competing.

Argentina, Brazil, Uruguay, Paraguay and the USA with 6 ex-British professionals were seeded, the last two named countries being drawn in the same group.

Construction of the Centenario Stadium began in February but despite day and night work it remained unfinished at the start because of intermittent heavy rain. Early games were played on other grounds.

Argentina's matches were eventful. 5 penalties were awarded in the game with Mexico, and against France the referee ended proceedings 6 minutes prematurely, leaving mounted police to clear the pitch for the remaining minutes to be played.

The worst incident involved Chile when Argentina's centre-half Luisito Monti committed a foul which sparked a players' free-for-all and required the police to restore order.

When Argentina reached the final, many of their fans chartered boats across the River Plate and were frisked for weapons on arrival. They were to lose to Uruguay, however, in a match refereed by the Belgian John Langenus resplendent in cap and bloomer-like plus fours.

1930 GROUP 1

13.7.30 **France** (3) **4 Mexico** (0) 1 *Montevideo*

France: Thepot; Mattler, Capelle, Villaplane, Pinel, Chantrel, Liberati, Delfour, Maschinot (2), Laurent (1), Langiller (1)
Mexico: Bonfiglio; Gutierrez R., Rosas M., Rosas F., Sanchez, Amezcua, Perez, Carreno (1), Mejia, Ruiz, Lopez *Referee:* Lombardi (Uruguay)

On 13 July 1930 Louis Laurent of France became the scorer of the first World Cup goal in a 4-1 win over Mexico.

15.7.30 **Argentina** (0) 1 **France** (0) 0 *Montevideo*

Argentina: Bossio; Della Torre, Muttis, Suarez, Monti (1), Evaristo J., Perinetti, Varallo, Ferreyra, Gierro, Evaristo M.
France: as 13.7.30. *Referee:* Rego (Brazil)

16.7.30 **Chile** (1) 3 **Mexico** (0) 0 *Montevideo*

Chile: Cortes; Morales, Porier, Torres A., Saavedra, Helgueta, Ojeda, Subiabre (2), Villalobos, Vidal (1), Scheuerberger
Mexico: Sota; Gutierrez R, Rosas M., Rosas F., Sanchez, Amezcua, Perez, Carreno, Ruiz, Gayon, Lopez *Referee:* Christophe (Belgium)

19.7.30 **Chile** (0) 1 **France** (0) 0 *Montevideo*

Chile: Cortes; Ciaparro, Morales, Torres A., Saavedra, Torres C., Ojeda, Subiabre (1), Villalobos, Vidal, Scheuerberger
France: Thepot; Mattler, Capelle, Chantrel, Delmer, Villaplane, Liberati, Delfour, Pinel, Veinante, Langiller *Referee:* Tejada (Uruguay)

19.7.30 **Argentina** (3) 6 **Mexico** (1) 3 *Montevideo*

Argentina: Bossio; Della Torre, Paternoster, Cividini, Zumelzu (2 pens.), Orlandini, Peucelle, Varallo (1), Stabile (3), Demaria, Spadaro
Mexico: Bonfiglio; Gutierrez R., Gutierrez F., Rosas M. (2 pens.), Sanchez, Rodriguez, Rosas F, Lopez (1), Gayon, Carreno, Olivares
Referee: Saucedo (Bolivia)

22.7.30 **Argentina** (2) 3 **Chile** (1) 1 *Montevideo*

Argentina: Bossio; Della Torre, Paternoster, Evaristo J., Monti, Orlandini, Peucelle, Varallo, Stabile (2), Ferreyra, Evaristo M. (1)
Chile: Cortes; Ciaparro, Morales, Torres A., Saavedra, Torres C., Avellane, Subiabre (1), Villalobos, Vidal, Aquilera *Referee:* Langenus (Belgium)

	P	W	D	L	F	A	Pts
Argentina	3	3	0	0	10	4	6
Chile	3	2	0	1	5	3	4
France	3	1	0	2	4	3	2
Mexico	3	0	0	3	4	13	0

GROUP 2

14.7.30 **Yugoslavia** (2) 2 **Brazil** (0) 1 *Montevideo*

Yugoslavia: Jaksic; Ivkovic, Mihailovic, Arsenijevic, Stefanovic, Dokic, Tirnanic (1), Marjanovic (1), Beck, Vujadinovic, Sekulic
Brazil: Joel; Brilhante, Italia, Hermogenes, Fausto, Fernando, Poly, Nilo, Araken, Preguinho (1), Moderato *Referee:* Tejada (Uruguay)

17.7.30 **Yugoslavia** (0) **4 Bolivia** (0) 0 *Montevideo*

Yugoslavia: Jaksic; Ivkovic, Mihailovic, Arsenijevic, Stefanovic, Dokic, Tirnanic, Marjanovic (1), Beck (2), Vujadinovic (1), Najdanovic
Bolivia: Bermudez; Durandal, Ciavarria, Argote, Lara, Valderrama, Gomez, Bustamante, Mendez, Alborta, Fernandez *Referee:* Mateucci (Mexico)

20.7.30 **Brazil** (1) **4 Bolivia** (0) 0 *Montevideo*

Brazil: Velloso; Ze Luiz, Italia, Hermogenes, Fausto, Fernando, Benedito, Russinho, Leite, Preguinho (2), Moderato (2)
Bolivia: Bermudez; Durandal, Ciavarria, Sainz, Lara, Valderrama, Ortiz, Bustamante, Mendez, Alborta, Fernandez *Referee:* Balway (France)

	P	W	D	L	F	A	Pts
Yugoslavia	2	2	0	0	6	1	4
Brazil	2	1	0	1	5	2	2
Bolivia	2	0	0	2	0	8	0

GROUP 3

14.7.30 **Rumania** (1) 3 **Peru** (0) 1 *Montevideo*

Rumania: Lapusneanu; Steiner, Burger, Rafinski, Vogl, Fieraru, Covaci, Desu, Wetzer, Staucin (2), Barbu (1)
Peru: Valdiviso; De las Casas, Soria, Galindo, Garcia, Valle, Flores, Villanueva, Denegri, Neira, Souza (1) *Referee:* Warken (Chile)

The lowest attendance for a match in the World Cup final tournament was probably 300 for the Rumania v Peru game on July 14, 1930 in Montevideo, Uruguay. The highest: 199,850 was for Brazil v Uruguay on July 16, 1950, Rio de Janeiro, Brazil.

18.7.30 **Uruguay** (0) 1 **Peru** (0) 0 *Montevideo*

Uruguay: Ballesteros; Nasazzi, Tejera, Andrade, Fernandez, Gestido, Urdinaran, Castro (1), Petrone, Cea, Iriarte
Peru: Pardon; De las Casas, Maquillon, Denegri, Galindo, Astengo, Lavalle, Flores, Villanueva, Neira, Souza *Referee:* Langenus (Belgium)

21.7.30 **Uruguay** (3) **4 Rumania** (0) 0 *Montevideo*

Uruguay: Ballesteros; Nasazzi, Mascheroni, Andrade, Fernandez, Gestido, Dorado (1), Scarone (1), Anselmo (1), Cea (1), Iriarte
Rumania: Lapusneanu; Burger, Tacu, Robl. Vogl, Fieraru, Covaci, Desu, Wetzer, Rafinski, Barbu *Referee:* Rego (Brazil)

	P	W	D	L	F	A	Pts
Uruguay	2	2	0	0	5	0	4
Rumania	2	1	0	1	3	5	2
Peru	2	0	0	2	1	4	0

GROUP 4

13.7.30 **USA** (2) 3 **Belgium** (0) 0 *Montevideo*

USA: Douglas; Wood, Moorhouse, Gallacher, Tracey, Brown, Gonzalvez, Florie, Patenaude (1), Auld, McGhee (2)
Belgium: Badjou; Nouwens, Hoydonckx, Braine, Hellemans, Declercq, Diddens, Moeschal, Adams, Voorhoof, Versijp *Referee:* Macias (Argentina)

17.7.30 **USA** (2) 3 **Paraguay** (0) 0 *Montevideo*

USA: as 13.7.30, Patenaude (2), Florie (1)
Paraguay: Denis; Olmedo, Miracca, Etcheverrey, Diaz, Aguirre, Nessi, Dominguez, Gonzales, Gaceres, Pena *Referee:* Macias (Argentina)

20.7.30 **Paraguay** (1) 1 **Belgium** (0) 0 *Montevideo*

Paraguay: Benitez P; Olmedo, Flores, Benitez S., Diaz, Garcete, Nessi, Romero, Gonzales, Gaceres, Pena (1)
Belgium: Badjou; Dedeken, Hoydonckx, Braine, Hellemans, Moeschal, Versijp, Delbeke, Adams, Nouwens, Diddens *Referee:* Vallarino (Uruguay)

	P	W	D	L	F	A	Pts
USA	2	2	0	0	6	0	4
Paraguay	2	1	0	1	1	3	2
Belgium	2	0	0	2	0	4	0

SEMI-FINALS

26.7.30 **Argentina** (1) 6 **USA** (0) 1 *Montevideo*

Argentina: Botasso; Della Torre, Paternoster, Evaristo J., Monti (2), Orlandini, Peucelle, Scopelli (2), Stabile (2), Ferreyra, Evaristo M.
USA: as 13.7.30, Brown (1) *Referee:* Langenus (Belgium)

27.7.30 **Uruguay** (3) 6 **Yugoslavia** (1) 1 *Montevideo*

Uruguay: as 21.7.30, Anselmo (2), Cea (3), Iriarte (1)
Yugoslavia: as 14.7.30, Sekulic (1) *Referee:* Rego (Brazil)

FINAL

30.7.30 **Uruguay** (1) **4 Argentina** (2) 2 *Montevideo* Attendance: 90,000

Uruguay: Ballesteros; Nasazzi, Mascheroni, Andrade, Gestido, Fernandez, Dorado (1), Scarone, Castro (1), Cea (1), Iriarte (1)
Argentina: Botasso; Della Torre, Paternoster, Evaristo J., Monti, Suarez, Peucelle (1), Varallo, Stabile (1), Ferreyra, Evaristo M.
Referee: Langenus (Belgium)

1934

31 entries boosted the finals in Italy. There were 10 regional qualifying groups producing 16 finalists in a knock-out competition, though 8 countries were seeded.

8 venues were used and the hosts, under the Fascist regime of Mussolini, extracted maximum propaganda value from what proved a well organised operation.

Italy's manager Vittorio Pozzo was a shrewd leader, admirably controlling his temperamental team which included 3 ex-Argentines, including Monti.

Uruguay, annoyed by Europe's apparent snub 4 years previously, did not enter and Argentina, fearing a further loss of players, sent a weakened side.

Weak refereeing contributed to the disintegration of the Spain v Italy match. 7 Spaniards and 4 Italians were injured (1 Italian breaking his leg). The replay was quieter, but again poorly handled.

The Italians eventually reached the final despite having had to play 3 matches in 4 days. Special trains, motor coaches and cars carried Czechoslovakian fans across the Alps for it, but the Italians won in extra time.

1934 PRELIMINARY ROUND

27.5.34 **Italy** (3) 7 **USA** (0) 1 *Rome*

Italy: Combi; Rosetta, Allemandi, Pizzioli, Monti, Bertolini, Guarisi, Meazza (1), Schiavio (3), Ferrari (1), Orsi (2)
USA: Hjulian; Czerkiewicz, Moorhouse, Pietras, Gonzalvez, Florie, Ryan, Nilson, Donelli (1), Dick, MacLean *Referee:* Mercet (Switzerland)

27.5.34 **Czechoslovakia** (0) 2 **Rumania** (1) 1 *Trieste*

Czechoslovakia: Planicka; Zenizek, Ctyroky, Kostalek, Cambal, Krcil, Junek, Silny, Sobotka, Nejedly (1), Puc (1)
Rumania: Zambori; Vogl, Albu, Deheleanu, Cotormani, Moravet, Bindea, Covaci, Sepi, Bodola, Dobai (1) *Referee:* Langenus (Belgium)

27.5.34 **Spain** (3) 3 **Brazil** (0) 1 *Genoa*

Spain: Zamora; Ciriaco, Quincoces, Cilaurren, Muquerza, Marculeta, Lafuente, Iraragorri (pen.), Langara (2), Lecue, Gorostiza
Brazil: Pedrosa; Sylvio, Luz, Tinoco, Martim, Armandinho, Canalli, Luizinho, Waldemar, Patesko, Leonidas (1) *Referee:* Birlem (Germany)

27.5.34 **Switzerland** (2) 3 **Netherlands** (1) 2 *Milan*

Switzerland: Sechehaye; Minelli, Weiler II, Guinchard, Jaccard, Hufschmid, Von Kanel, Passello, Kielholz (2), Abegglen III (1), Bossi
Netherlands: Van der Meulen; Weber, Van Run, Pellikaan, Anderiesen, Van Heel, Wels, Vente (1), Bakhuijs, Smit (1), Van Nellen
Referee: Eklind (Sweden)

Refereeing can be a monstrous undertaking. In 1934 and 1937 two World Cup qualifying matches involving Hungary and Bulgaria, and Lithuania and Latvia respectively were controlled by Herr Frankenstein of Austria.

27.5.34 **Sweden** (1) 3 **Argentina** (1) 2 *Bologna*

Sweden: Rydberg; Axelsson, Andersson S., Carlsson, Rosen, Andersson E., Dunker, Gustavsson, Jonasson (2), Keller, Kroon (1)
Argentina: Freschi; Pedevilla, Belis (1), Nehin, Sosa-Ubrieta, Lopez, Rua, Wilde, De Vincenzi, Galateo (1), Iraneta *Referee:* Braun (Austria)

27.5.34 **Germany** (1) 5 **Belgium** (2) 2 *Florence*

Germany: Kress; Haringer, Schwartz, Janes, Szepan, Zielinski, Lehner, Hohmann, Conen (3), Siffling, Kobierski (2)
Belgium: Van de Weyer; Smellinckx, Joachim, Peeraer, Welkenhuyzen, Klaessens, Devries, Voorhoof (2), Capelle, Gimmonprez, Herremans
Referee: Mattea (Italy)

27.5.34 **Austria** (1) 3 **France** (1) 2 *Turin*
(after extra time; 1-1 at 90 mins)

Austria: Platzer; Cisar, Sesta, Wagner, Smistik, Urbanek, Zischek, Bican (1), Sindelar (1), Schall (1), Viertel
France: Thepot; Mairesse, Mattler, Delfour, Verriest (pen.), Llense, Keller, Alcazar, Nicolas (1), Rio, Aston
Referee: Van Moorsel (Netherlands)

27.5.34 **Hungary** (2) **4 Egypt** (2) 2 *Naples*

Hungary: Szabo A; Futo, Sternberg, Palotas, Szucs, Lazar, Markos, Vincze (1), Teleki (1), Toldi (2), Szabo F.
Egypt: Moustafa Kemal; Ali Caf, Hamitu, El Far, Refaat, Rayab, Latif, Fawzi (2), Muktar, Masoud Kemal, Hassan
Referee: Barlassina (Italy)

QUARTER-FINALS

31.5.34 **Germany** (0) 2 **Sweden** (0) 1 *Milan*

Germany: Kress; Haringer, Busch, Gramlich, Szepan, Zielinski, Lehner, Hohmann (2), Conen, Siffling, Kobierski
Sweden: as 27.5.34 Dunker (1) *Referee:* Barlassina (Italy)

31.5.34 **Czechoslovakia** (1) 3 **Switzerland** (1) 2 *Turin*

Czechoslovakia: Planicka; Zenizek, Ctyroky, Kostalek, Cambal, Krcil, Junek, Svoboda (1), Sobotka (1), Nejedly (1), Puc
Switzerland: Sechehaye; Minelli, Weiler II, Guinchard, Jaccard, Hufschmid, Von Kanel, Jaeggi IV, Kielholz (1), Abegglen III (1), Jack
Referee: Beranek (Austria)

31.5.34 **Austria** (1) 2 **Hungary** (0) 1 *Bologna*

Austria: Platzer; Cisar, Sesta, Wagner, Smistik, Urbanek, Zischek (1), Bican, Sindelar, Horvath (1), Viertel
Hungary: Szabo A; Vago, Sternberg, Palotas, Szucs, Szalay, Markos, Avar, Sarosi (pen.), Toldi, Kemeny *Referee:* Mattea (Italy)

31.5.34 **Italy** (0) 1 **Spain** (1) 1 (1-1 at 90 mins) *Florence*

Italy: Combi; Monzeglio, Allemandi, Pizziolo, Monti, Castellazzi, Guaita, Meazza, Schiavio, Ferrari (1), Orsi
Spain: Zamora; Ciriaco, Quincoces, Cillaurren, Muquerza, Lecue, Lafuente, Iraragorri, Langara, Regueiro (1), Gorostiza *Referee:* Baert (Belgium)

1.6.34 **(replay) Italy** (1) 1 **Spain** (0) 0 *Florence*

Italy: Combi; Monzeglio, Allemandi, Ferraris IV, Monti, Bertolini, Guaita, Meazza (1), Borel II, Demaria, Orsi
Spain: Nogues; Zabalo, Quincoces, Cillaurren, Muquerza, Lecue, Ventolra, Regueiro, Campanal, Chacha, Bosch *Referee:* Mercet (Switzerland)

SEMI-FINALS

3.6.34 **Czechoslovakia** (1) 3 **Germany** (0) 1 *Rome*

Czechoslovakia: Planicka; Ctyroky, Burger, Kostalek, Cambal, Krcil (1), Junek, Svoboda, Sobotka, Nejedly (2), Puc
Germany: Kress; Busch, Haringer, Zielinski, Szepan, Bender, Lehner, Siffling, Conen, Noack (1), Kobierski *Referee:* Barlassina (Italy)

3.6.34 **Italy** (1) 1 **Austria** (0) 0 *Milan*

Italy: Combi; Monzeglio, Allemandi, Ferraris IV, Monti, Bertolini, Guaita (1), Meazza, Schiavio, Ferrari, Orsi
Austria: as 27.5.34. *Referee:* Eklind (Sweden)

MATCH FOR THIRD PLACE

6.6.34 **Germany** (3) 3 **Austria** (1) 2 *Naples*

Germany: Jakob; Janes, Busch, Zielinski, Munzenberg, Bender, Lehner (2), Siffling, Conen (1), Szepan, Heidemann
Austria: Platzer; Cisar, Sesta (1), Wagner, Smistik, Urbanek, Zischek, Braun, Bican, Horvath (1), Viertel *Referee:* Carraro (Italy)

FINAL

10.6.34 **Italy** (0) 2 **Czechoslovakia** (0) 1 *Rome* Attendance: 50,000
(after extra time; 1-1 at 90 mins)

Italy: as semi-final, Schiavio (1), Orsi (1)
Czechoslovakia: as 31.5.34, Puc (1) *Referee:* Eklind (Sweden)

1938

The scent of war hung heavily over the finals in France as Italy (with just 2 survivors from 1934) retained their title.

Again 8 teams were seeded in a 'sudden-death' system and for the first time both hosts and holders were exempted from qualifying. Of the 36 entries, 9 withdrew without playing while Rumania, Brazil, the Dutch East Indies and Cuba reached the final without kicking a ball. Argentina entered late then withdrew. Uruguay were again absent.

Spain were unable to compete because of the civil war. Austria qualified and were scheduled to meet Sweden at Lyon, whereupon FIFA were informed that owing to Germany's annexation of their country, Austria would not after all be competing. Sweden had a walkover and 4 of the Austrians ended up playing for Germany.

Brazil beat Poland 6–5 after extra time, the Poles equalising no less than 3 times. In a drawn game against Czechoslovakia, the Brazilians were involved in a fracas, 2 of their players being sent off with a Czech, whose team lost 2 more men with fractures.

For the replay Brazil prevailed after making 9 changes to the Czechs' 6. But, over-confidently, they omitted key players against Italy and lost.

Though there was some local hostility towards them, the fast, sharp-shooting Italians finally outgunned Hungary.

1938 PRELIMINARY ROUND

4.6.38 **Switzerland** (1) 1 **Germany** (1) 1 (1-1 at 90 mins) Paris

Switzerland: Huber; Minelli, Lehmann, Springer, Vernati, Lortscher, Amado, Walaschek, Bickel, Abegglen III (1), Aeby
Germany: Raftl; Janes, Schmaus, Kupfer, Mock, Kitzinger, Lehner, Gellesch, Gauchel (1), Hahnemann, Pesser *Referee:* Langenus (Belgium)

4..6.38 **Hungary** (4) 6 **Dutch East Indies** (0) 0 *Reims*

Hungary: Hada; Koranyi, Biro, Lazar, Turai, Balogh, Sas, Zsengeller (2), Sarosi (2), Toldi (1), Kohut (1)
Dutch East Indies: Mo Heng; Hu Kon, Samuels, Nawir, Meng, Anwar, Hang Djin, Soedarmadji, Sommers, Pattiwael, Taihutti *Referee:* Conrie (France)

5.6.38 **France** (2) 3 **Belgium** (1) 1 *Paris*

France: Dilorto; Cazenave, Mattler, Bastien, Jordan, Diagne, Aston, Nicolas (2), Delfour, Veinante (1), Heisserer
Belgium: Badjou; Paverick, Sayes, Van Alphen, Stynen, De Winter, Van de Wouwer, Voorhoof, Isemborghs (1), Braine, Byle
Referee: Wuthrich (Switzerland)

5.6.38 **Brazil** (2) 6 **Poland** (1) 5 (**4-4** at 90 mins) *Strasbourg*

Brazil: Batatais; Domingos, Machado, Zeze Procopio, Martim, Afonsinho, Lopes, Romeu (1), Leonidas (4), Peracio (1), Hercules
Poland: Madejski; Szcepaniak, Galecki, Gora, Nyc, Dytko, Piecc I, Piontek (1), Szerfke, Willimowski (4), Wodarz *Referee:* Eklind (Sweden)

5.6.38 **Czechoslovakia** (0) 3 **Netherlands** (0) 0 *Le Havre*
(after extra time; 0-0 at 90 mins)

Czechoslovakia: Planicka; Burger, Daucik, Kostalek (1), Boucek (1), Kopecky, Riha, Simunek, Zeman, Nejedly (1), Puc
Netherlands: Van Male; Weber, Caldenhove, Paauwe, Anderiesen, Van Heel, Wels, Van de Veen, Smit, Vente, De Harder *Referee:* Leclerq (France)

5.6.38 **Italy** (1) 2 **Norway** (0) 1 (1-1 at 90 mins) *Marseilles*

Italy: Olivieri; Monzeglio, Rava, Serantoni, Andreolo, Locatelli, Pasinati, Meazza, Piola (1), Ferrari, Ferraris II (1)
Norway: Johansen H; Johannesen R., Holmsen, Henriksen, Eriksen, Homberg, Frantzen, Kvammen, Brunyldsen, Isaksen, Brustad (1)
Referee: Beranek (Austria)

5.6.38 **Cuba** (1) 3 **Rumania** (1) 3 (2-2 at 90 mins) *Toulouse*

Cuba: Carvajales; Barquin, Chorens, Arias, Rodriguez, Berges, Maquina (1), Fernandez, Socorro, Tunas (1), Sosa (1)
Rumania: Pavlovici; Burger, Chiroiu, Vintila, Rasinaru, Rafinski, Bindea, Covaci (1), Baratki (1), Bodola, Dobai (1) *Referee:* Scarpi (Italy)

9.6.38 **(replay) Switzerland** (1) 4 **Germany** (2) 2 *Paris*

Switzerland: Huber; Minelli, Lehmann, Springer, Vernati, Lortscher (o.g.), Amado, Abegglen III (2), Bickel (1), Walaschek (1), Aeby
Germany: Raftl; Janes, Streitle, Kupfer, Goldbrunner, Skoumal, Lehner, Stroh, Hahnemann (1), Szepan, Neumer *Referee:* Eklind (Sweden)

9.6.38 **(replay) Cuba** (0) 2 **Rumania** (1) 1 *Toulouse*

Cuba: Ayra; Barquin, Chorens, Arias, Rodriguez, Berges, Maquina (1), Fernandez, Socorro (1), Tunas, Sosa
Rumania: Sadowski; Burger, Felecan, Barbulescu, Racinaru, Rafinski, Bogden, Moldoveanu, Baratki, Pranzler, Dobai (1)
Referee: Birlem (Germany)

QUARTER-FINALS

12.6.38 **Sweden (4) 8 Cuba** (0) 0 *Antibes*

Sweden: Abrahamsson; Eriksson, Kallgren, Almgren, Jacobsson, Svanstrom, Wetterstrom (4), Keller (1), Andersson H. (1), Jonasson (1), Nyberg (1)
Cuba: Carvajales; Barquin, Chorens, Arias, Rodriguez, Berges, Ferrer, Fernandez, Socorro, Tunas, Alonzo *Referee:* Krist (Czechoslovakia)

12.6.38 **Hungary** (1) 2 **Switzerland** (0) 0 *Lille*

Hungary: Szabo; Koranyi, Biro, Szalay, Turai, Lazar, Sas, Vincze, Sarosi, Zsengeller (2), Kohut
Switzerland: Huber; Stelzer, Lehmann, Springer, Vernati, Lortscher, Amado, Walashek, Bickel, Abegglen III, Grassi *Referee:* Barlassina (Italy)

12.6.38 **Italy** (1) 3 **France** (1) 1 *Paris*

Italy: Olivieri; Foni, Rava, Serantoni, Andreolo, Locatelli, Biavati, Meazza, Piola (2), Ferrari, Colaussi (1)
France: Dilorto; Cazenave, Mattler, Bastien, Jordan, Diagne, Aston, Heisserer (1), Nicolas, Delfour, Veinante *Referee:* Baert (Belgium)

12.6.38 **Brazil** (1) 1 **Czechoslovakia** (1) 1 (1-1 at 90 mins) *Bordeaux*

Brazil: Walter; Domingos, Machado, Zeze Procopio, Martim, Afonsinho, Lopes, Romeu, Leonidas (1), Peracio, Hercules
Czechoslovakia: Planicka; Burger, Daucik, Kostalek, Boucek, Kopecky, Riha, Simunek, Ludl, Nejedly (pen.), Puc *Referee:* Hertzka (Hungary)

14.6.38 **(replay) Brazil** (0) 2 **Czechoslovakia** (1) 1 *Bordeaux*

Brazil: Walter; Jau, Nariz, Brito, Brandao, Argemiro, Roberto (1), Luizinho, Leonidas (1), Tim, Patesko
Czechoslovakia: Burkert; Burger, Daucik, Kostalek, Boucek, Ludl, Horak, Senecky, Kreutz, Kopecky (1), Rulc *Referee:* Capdeville (France)

Fastest goals scored in the competition: Olle Nyberg, 30 seconds (Sweden v Hungary 1938) and Bernard Lacombe, 31 seconds (France v Italy 1978).

SEMI-FINALS

16.6.38 **Italy** (0) 2 **Brazil** (0) 1 *Marseilles*

Italy: Olivieri; Foni, Rava, Serantoni, Andreolo, Locatelli, Biavati, Meazza (pen.), Piola, Ferrari, Colaussi (1)
Brazil: Walter; Domingos, Machado, Zeze Procopio, Martim, Afonsinho, Lopes, Luizinho, Peracio, Romeu (1), Patesko
Referee: Wuthrich (Switzerland)

16.6.38 **Hungary** (3) 5 **Sweden** (1) 1 *Paris*

Hungary: Szabo; Koranyi, Biro, Szalay, Turai, Lazar, Sas, Zsengeller (3), Sarosi (1), Toldi, Titkos (1)
Sweden: Abrahamsson; Eriksson, Kallgren, Almgren, Jacobsson, Svanstrom, Wetterstrom, Keller, Andersson H., Jonasson, Nyberg (1)
Referee: Leclerq (France)

MATCH FOR THIRD PLACE

19.6.38 **Brazil** (1) **4 Sweden** (2) 2 *Bordeaux*

Brazil: Batatais; Domingos, Machado, Zeze Procopio, Brandao, Afonsinho, Roberto, Romeu (1), Leonidas (2), Peracio (1), Patesko
Sweden: Abrahamsson, Eriksson, Nilsson, Almgren, Linderholm, Svanstrom, Persson, Andersson H., Jonasson (1), Andersson A., Nyberg (1) *Referee:* Langenus (Belgium)

FINAL

19.6.38 **Italy** (3) **4 Hungary** (1) 2 *Paris* Attendance: 45,000

Italy: as semi-final, Piola (2), Colaussi (2)
Hungary: Szabo; Polgar, Biro, Szalay, Szucs, Lazar, Sas, Vincze, Sarosi (1), Zsengeller, Titkos (1) *Referee:* Capdeville (France)

1950

England players trained at Ascot but finished as also-rans in Brazil, humiliated by the USA who had played together only twice previously. The matches were saddled with other shocks with the hosts and 10–1 on favourites Brazil also coming unstuck.

Though there were 32 entries a combination of factors led to just 13 finalists. Scotland snubbed a final place after losing to England in the British International Championship, used as part of the qualification.

Turkey played then withdrew, while Austria (who had been scheduled to meet the Turks) also pulled out, as did Belgium before meeting Switzerland. India, threatened with disqualification if they attempted to play bare-footed, also withdrew. France, who had been eliminated by Yugoslavia, were then invited to compete but also declined.

Bolivia, Chile, Uruguay and Paraguay reached the finals without playing. Uruguay actually found themselves in a group consisting of just one opponent and inevitably profited from it.

The group winners met in a final pool. There was no actual final though the last game between Brazil and winners Uruguay was the deciding one. It was staged at the giant Maracana Stadium in Rio, uncompleted despite 6,500 men working on it 24 hours a day.

1950 GROUP 1

24.6.50 **Brazil** (1) **4 Mexico** (0) 0 *Rio de Janeiro*

Brazil: Barbosa; Augusto, Juvenal, Ely, Danilo, Bigode, Maneca, Ademir (2), Baltazar (1), Jair (1), Friaca
Mexico: Carbajal; Zetter, Montemajor, Ruiz, Ochoa, Roca, Septien, Ortiz, Casarin, Perez, Velasquez *Referee:* Reader (England)

25.6.50 **Yugoslavia** (3) 3 **Switzerland** (0) 0 *Belo Horizonte*

Yugoslavia: Mrkusic; Horvat, Stankovic, Cajkovski I, Jovanovic, Djajic, Ognanov (1), Mitic, Tomasevic (2), Bobek, Vukas
Switzerland: Stuber; Lusenti, Quinche, Bocquet, Eggimann, Neury, Bickel, Antenen, Tamini, Bader, Fatton *Referee:* Galeati (Italy)

28.6.50 **Brazil** (2) 2 **Switzerland** (1) 2 *Sao Paulo*

Brazil: Barbosa; Augusto, Juvenal, Bauer, Rui, Noronha, Alfredo II (1), Maneca, Baltazar (1), Ademir, Friaca
Switzerland: Stuber; Neury, Bocquet, Lusenti, Eggimann, Quinche, Tamini, Bickel, Friedlander, Bader, Fatton (2) *Referee:* Azon (Spain)

28.6.50 **Yugoslavia** (2) **4 Mexico** (0) 1 *Porto Alegre*

Yugoslavia: as 25.6.50, Bobek (1), Cajkovski I (2), Tomasevic (1)
Mexico: Carbajal; Gutierrez, Ruiz, Gomez, Ochoa, Ortiz, Flores, Naranjo, Casarin (1), Perez, Velasquez *Referee:* Leafe (England)

1.7.50 **Brazil** (1) 2 **Yugoslavia** (0) 0 *Rio de Janeiro*

Brazil: Barbosa; Augusto, Juvenal, Bauer, Danilo, Bigode, Maneca, Zizinho (1), Ademir (1), Jair, Chico
Yugoslavia: Mrkusic; Horvat, Brokela, Cajkovski I, Jovanovic, Djajic, Vukas, Mitic, Tomasevic, Bobek, Cajkovski II *Referee:* Griffiths (Wales)

2.7.50 **Switzerland** (2) 2 **Mexico** (0) 1 *Porto Alegre*

Switzerland: Hug; Neury, Bocquet, Lusenti, Eggimann, Quinche, Tamini, Antenen, Friedlander, Bader (1), Fatton (1)
Mexico: Carbajal; Gutierrez, Gomez, Roca, Ortiz, Guevara, Flores, Ochoa, Casarin, Borbolla, Velasquez (1) *Referee:* Eklind (Sweden)

Antonio Carbajal is the only player to have appeared in as many as 5 World Cup final tournaments. He kept goal for Mexico in the 1950, 1954, 1958, 1962 and 1966 competitions, making 11 appearances in all.

	P	W	D	L	F	A	Pts
Brazil	3	2	1	0	8	2	5
Yugoslavia	3	2	0	1	7	3	4
Switzerland	3	1	1	1	4	6	3
Mexico	3	0	0	3	2	10	0

GROUP 2

24.6.50 **England** (1) 2 **Chile** (0) 0 *Rio de Janeiro*

England: Williams; Ramsey, Aston, Wright, Hughes, Dickinson, Finney, Mortensen (1), Bentley, Mannion (1), Mullen
Chile: Livingstone; Farias, Roldon, Alvarez, Busquets, Carvalho, Prieto, Cremaschi, Robledo, Munoz, Dias *Referee:* Van de Meer (Netherlands)

25.6.50 **Spain** (0) 3 **USA** (1) 1 *Curitiba*

Spain: Eizaguirre; Antunez, Alonso, Gonzalvo III, Gonzalvo II, Puchades, Basora (2), Hernandez, Zarra (1), Igoa, Gainza
USA: Borghi; Keough, Marca, McIlvenny, Colombo, Bahr, Craddock, Souza J. (1), Gaetjens, Pariani, Valentini *Referee:* Viana (Brazil)

29.6.50 **USA** (1) 1 **England** (0) 0 *Belo Horizonte*

USA: Borghi; Keough, Marca, McIlvenny, Colombo, Bahr, Wallace, Pariani, Gaetjens (1), Souza J., Souza E.
England: as 24.6.50. *Referee:* Dattilo (Italy)

29.6.50 **Spain** (2) 2 **Chile** (0) 0 *Rio de Janeiro*

Spain: Ramallets; Alonso, Parra, Gonzalvo III, Gonzalvo II, Puchades, Basora (1), Igoa, Zarra (1), Panizo, Gainza
Chile: Livingstone; Farias, Roldon, Alvarez, Busqueta, Carvalho, Prieto, Cremaschi, Robledo, Munoz, Diaz *Referee:* De Gama (Brazil)

2.7.50 **Spain** (0) 1 **England** (0) 0 *Rio de Janeiro*

Spain: as 29.6.50, Zarra (1)
England: Williams; Ramsey, Eckersley, Wright, Hughes, Dickinson, Matthews, Mortensen, Milburn, Baily, Finney *Referee:* Galeati (Italy)

2.7.50 **Chile** (2) 5 **USA** (0) 2 *Recife*

Chile: Livingstone; Machuca, Roldon, Alvarez, Busquets, Farias, Munoz, Cremaschi (3), Robledo (1), Prieto (1), Ibanez
USA: as 29.6.50, Pariani (1), Souza J. (pen.) *Referee:* Gardelli (Brazil)

	P	W	D	L	F	A	Pts
Spain	3	3	0	0	6	1	6
England	3	1	0	2	2	2	2
Chile	3	1	0	2	5	6	2
USA	3	1	0	2	4	8	2

GROUP 3

25.6.50 **Sweden** (2) 3 **Italy** (1) 2 *Sao Paulo*

Sweden: Svensson; Samuelsson, Nilsson E., Andersson (1), Nordahl K., Gaerd, Sundqvist, Palmer, Jeppson (2), Skoglund, Nilsson S.
Italy: Sentimenti IV; Giovannini, Furiassi, Annovazzi, Parola, Magli, Muccinelli (1), Boniperti, Cappello, Campatelli, Carapellese (1)
Referee: Lutz (Switzerland)

29.6.50 **Sweden** (2) 2 **Paraguay** (0) 2 *Curitiba*

Sweden: Svensson; Samuelsson, Nilsson E., Andersson, Nordahl K., Gaerd, Jonsson, Palmer (1), Jeppson, Skoglund, Sundqvist (1)
Paraguay: Vargas; Gonzalito, Cespedes, Gavilan, Lequizamon, Cantero, Avalos, Lopez A. (1), Saquir, Lopez F. (1), Unzain
Referee: Mitchell (Scotland)

2.7.50 **Italy** (1) 2 **Paraguay** (0) 0 *Sao Paulo*

Italy: Moro; Blason, Furiassi, Fattori, Remondini, Mari, Muccinelli, Pandolfini (1), Amadei, Capello, Carapellese (1)
Paraguay: Vargas; Gonzales, Cespedes, Gavilan, Lequizamon, Cantero, Avalos, Lopez A., Saquir, Lopez F., Unzain *Referee:* Ellis (England)

	P	W	D	L	F	A	Pts
Sweden	2	1	1	0	5	4	3
Italy	2	1	0	1	4	3	2
Paraguay	2	0	1	1	2	4	1

GROUP 4

2.7.50 **Uruguay** (4) 8 **Bolivia** (0) 0 *Belo Horizonte*

Uruguay: Maspoli; Gonzales M., Tejera, Gonzales J., Varela, Andrade, Ghigga (1), Perez, Miguez (2), Schiaffino (4), Vidal (1)
Bolivia: Gutierrez I; Acha, Bustamante, Greco, Valencia, Ferrel, Algranaz, Ugarte, Caparelli, Gutierrez II, Maldonado *Referee:* Reader (England)

	P	W	D	L	F	A	Pts
Uruguay	1	1	0	0	8	0	2
Bolivia	1	0	0	1	0	8	0

FINAL ROUND

9.7.50 **Brazil** (3) 7 **Sweden** (0) 1 *Rio de Janeiro*

Brazil: as 1.7.50, Maneca (1), Ademir (4), Chico (2)
Sweden: as 25.6.50, Andersson (pen.) *Referee:* Ellis (England)

9.7.50 **Uruguay** (1) 2 **Spain** (2) 2 *Sao Paulo*

Uruguay: as 2.7.50, Varela (1), Chiggia (1)
Spain: Ramallets; Alonso, Gonzalvo II, Gonzalvo III, Parra, Puchades, Basora (2), Igoa, Zarra, Molowny, Gainza *Referee:* Griffiths (Wales)

13.7.50 **Brazil** (3) 6 **Spain** (0) 1 *Rio de Janeiro*

Brazil: Barbosa; Augusto, Juvenal, Bauer, Danilo, Bigode, Friaca, Zizinho (2), Ademir, Jair (2), Chico (2)
Spain: as 29.6.50, Igoa (1) *Referee:* Leafe (England)

13.7.50 **Uruguay** (1) 3 **Sweden** (2) 2 *Sao Paulo*

Uruguay: Paz; Gonzales M., Tejera, Gambetta, Varela, Andrade, Ghiggia, Perez (1), Miguez, Schiaffino (2), Vidal
Sweden: Svensson; Samuelsson, Nilsson E., Andersson, Johansson, Gaerd, Sundqvist, Palmer (1), Jeppson (1), Jonsson, Nilsson S.
Referee: Galeati (Italy)

16.7.50 **Sweden** (2) 3 **Spain** (0) 1 *Sao Paulo*

Sweden: Svensson; Samuelsson, Nilsson E., Andersson, Johansson, Gaerd, Jonsson, Mellberg (1), Rydell, Palmer (1), Sundqvist (1)
Spain: Eizaguirre; Alonso, Asensi, Silva, Parra, Puchades, Basora, Hernandez, Zarra (1), Paniza, Juncosa *Referee:* Van de Meer (Netherlands)

16.7.50 **Uruguay** (0) 2 **Brazil** (0) 1 *Rio de Janeiro* Attendance: 199,850

Uruguay: Maspoli; Gonzales M., Tejera, Gambetta, Varela, Andrade, Ghiggia (1), Perez, Miguez, Schiaffino (1), Moran
Brazil: as 13.7.50, Friaca (1) *Referee:* Reader (England)

	P	W	D	L	F	A	Pts
Uruguay	3	2	1	0	7	5	5
Brazil	3	2	0	1	14	4	4
Sweden	3	1	0	2	6	11	2
Spain	3	0	1	2	4	11	1

1954

The tournament in Switzerland produced both the most disgraceful scenes in the history of the competition and the finest exhibition of World Cup football. Both matches involved Hungary, the pre-series favourites.

The infamously belligerent Battle of Berne between Hungary and Brazil saw 3 players sent off, but the most deplorable incidents occurred in the dressing-room after the final whistle.

Hungary, though not the chief culprits, redeemed themselves in the memorable semi-final with Uruguay which, though fought out in torrential rain, was a privilege to watch for those of us present. Uruguay lost after extra time, their first defeat in the World Cup.

The Hungarians, unbeaten for 4 years, then bowed in the final to West Germany despite scoring 2 quick goals in another rain-drenched match.

Goalscoring reached a new peak as a result of at least a dozen teams possessing outstanding ability, an unsatisfactory system of two seeded teams per group and many poorer competitors.

West Germany's manager, Sepp Herberger cheekily exploited the flaws. With a deliberately weakened team, the Germans lost 8-3 to Hungary in a group game, then gambled on winning a play-off with Turkey which in turn led to their final success over the Hungarians.

1954 GROUP 1

16.6.54 **Yugoslavia** (1) 1 **France** (0) 0 *Lausanne*

Yugoslavia: Beara; Stankovic, Crnkovic, Cajkovski, Horvat, Boskov, Milutinovic (1), Mitic, Vukas, Bobek, Zebec
France: Remetter; Gianessi, Kaelbel, Penverne, Jonquet, Marcel, Kopa, Glovacki, Strappe, Dereudre, Vincent *Referee:* Griffiths (Wales)

16.6.54 **Brazil** (4) 5 **Mexico** (0) 0 *Geneva*

Brazil: Castilho; Santos D., Santos N., Brandaozinho, Pinheiro, Bauer, Julinho (1), Didi (1), Baltazar (1), Pinga (2), Rodrigues
Mexico: Mota; Lopez, Gomez, Cardenas, Romo, Avalos, Torres, Naranjo, Lamadrid, Balcazar, Arellano *Referee:* Wyssling (Switzerland)

19.6.54 **France** (1) 3 **Mexico** (0) 2 *Geneva*

France: Remetter; Gianessi, Marche, Marcel, Kaelbel, Mahjoub, Kopa (pen.), Dereudre, Strappe, Ben Tifour, Vincent (1)
Mexico: Carbajal; Lopez, Romo, Cardenas (o.g.), Avalos, Martinez, Torres, Naranjo (1), Lamadrid, Balcazar (1), Arellano *Referee:* Asensi (Spain)

19.6.54 **Brazil** (0) 1 **Yugoslavia** (0) 1 (1-1 at 90 mins) *Lausanne*

Brazil: as 16.6.54, Didi (1)
Yugoslavia: Beara; Stankovic, Crnkovic, Cajkovski I, Horvat, Boskov, Milutinovic, Mitic, Zebec (1), Vukas, Dvornik
Referee: Faultless (Scotland)

	P	W	D	L	F	A	Pts
Brazil	2	1	1	0	6	1	3
Yugoslavia	2	1	1	0	2	1	3
France	2	1	0	1	3	3	2
Mexico	2	0	0	2	2	8	0

GROUP 2

17.6.54 **Hungary** (4) 9 **South Korea** (0) 0 *Zurich*

Hungary: Grosics; Buzanszky, Lantos (1), Bozsik, Lorant, Szojka, Budai, Kocsis (3), Palotas (2), Puskas (2), Czibor (1)
South Korea: Hong; Kyu Park, Kang, Min, Yae Seung Park, Chu, Chung, Kap Park, Sung, Woo, Yung Keun Choi *Referee:* Vincenti (France)

17.6.54 **West Germany** (1) **4 Turkey** (1) 1 *Berne*

Germany: Turek; Laband, Kohlmeyer, Eckel, Posipal, Mai, Klodt (1), Morlock (1), Walter O. (1), Walter F., Schafer (1)
Turkey: Turgay; Ridvan, Basri, Mustafa, Cetin, Rober, Erol, Suat (1), Feridu, Burhan, Lefter *Referee:* Da Costa (Portugal)

20.6.54 **Hungary** (3) 8 **West Germany** (1) 3 *Basle*

Hungary: Grosics; Buzanszky, Lantos, Bozsik, Lorant, Zakarias, Toth (1), Kocsis (4), Hidegkuti (2), Puskas (1), Czibor
Germany: Kwaitkowski; Bauer, Kohlmeyer, Posipal, Liebrich, Mebus, Rahn (1), Eckel, Walter F., Pfaff (1), Hermann (1) *Referee:* Ling (England)

20.6.54 **Turkey** (4) 7 **South Korea** (0) 0 *Geneva*

Turkey: Turgay; Ridvan, Basri, Mustafa, Cetin, Rober, Erol (1), Suat (2), Necmettin, Lefter (1), Burhan (3)
South Korea: Hong; Kyu Park, Kang, Han, Chong Kap Lee, Kim, Yung Keun Choi, Soo Nam Lee, Gi Choo Lee, Woo, Chung
Referee: Marino (Uruguay)

	P	W	D	L	F	A	Pts
Hungary	2	2	0	0	17	3	4
West Germany	2	1	0	1	7	9	2
Turkey	2	1	0	1	8	4	2
South Korea	2	0	0	2	1	16	0

PLAY-OFF FOR 2nd PLACE

23.6.54 **West Germany** (3) 7 **Turkey** (1) 2 *Zurich*

Germany: Turek; Laband, Bauer, Eckel, Posipal, Mai, Klodt, Morlock (3), Walter O. (1), Walter F. (1), Schafer (2)
Turkey: Sukru; Ridvan, Basri, Naci, Cetin, Rober, Erol, Mustafa (1), Necmettin, Coskun, Lefter (1) *Referee:* Vincenti (France)

GROUP 3

16.6.54 **Austria** (1) 1 **Scotland** (0) 0 *Zurich*

Austria: Schmied; Hanappi, Barschandt, Ocwirk, Happel, Koller, Korner R., Schleger, Dienst, Probst (1), Korner A.
Scotland: Martin; Cunningham, Aird, Docherty, Davidson, Cowie, McKenzie, Fernie, Mochan, Brown, Ormond *Referee:* Franken (Belgium)

16.6.54 **Uruguay** (0) 2 **Czechoslovakia** (0) 0 *Berne*

Uruguay: Maspoli; Santamaria, Martinez, Andrade, Varela, Cruz, Abbadie, Ambrois, Miguez (1), Schiaffino (1), Borges
Czechoslovakia: Reimann; Safranek, Novak, Trnka, Hledlik, Hertl, Hlavacek, Hemele, Kacany, Pazicky, Peser *Referee:* Ellis (England)

19.6.54 **Austria** (4) 5 **Czechoslovakia** (0) 0 *Zurich*

Austria: Schmied; Hanappi, Barschandt, Ocwirk, Happel, Koller, Korner R., Wagner, Stojaspal (2), Probst (3), Korner A.
Czechoslovakia: Stacho; Safrenek, Novak, Trnka, Pluskal, Hertl, Hlavacek, Hemele, Kacany, Pazicky, Krauss *Referee:* Stefanovic (Yugoslavia)

19.6.54 **Uruguay** (2) 7 **Scotland** (0) 0 *Basle*

Uruguay: as 16.6.54, Abbadie (2), Miguez (2), Borges (3)
Scotland: as 16.6.54 *Referee:* Orlandini (Italy)

	P	W	D	L	F	A	Pts
Uruguay	2	2	0	0	9	0	**4**
Austria	2	2	0	0	6	0	**4**
Czechoslovakia	2	0	0	2	0	7	0
Scotland	2	0	0	2	0	8	0

GROUP 4

17.6.54 **England** (2) **4 Belgium** (1) **4** *Basle*
(after extra time; 3-3 at 90 mins)

England: Merrick; Staniforth, Byrne, Wright, Owen, Dickinson (o.g.), Matthews, Broadis (2), Lofthouse (2), Taylor, Finney
Belgium: Gernaey; Dries, Van Brandt, Huysmans, Carre, Mees, Van den Bosch, Houf, Coppens (1), Anoul (2), Mermans
Referee: Schmetzer (West Germany)

17.6.54 **Switzerland** (1) 2 **Italy** (1) 1 *Lausanne*

Switzerland: Parkier; Neury, Kernen, Fluckiger, Bocquet, Casali I, Ballaman (1), Vonlanthen, Hugi II (1), Meier, Fatton
Italy: Ghezzi; Vincenzi, Giacomazzi, Neri, Tognon, Nesti, Muccinelli, Boniperti (1), Galli, Pandolfini, Lorenzi
Referee: Viana (Brazil)

20.6.54 **England** (1) 2 **Switzerland** (0) *Berne*

England: Merrick; Staniforth, Byrne, McGarry, Wright, Dickinson, Finney, Broadis, Wilshaw (1), Taylor, Mullen (1)
Switzerland: Parlier; Neury, Kernen, Eggimann, Bocquet, Bigler, Antenen, Vonlanthen, Meier, Ballaman, Fatton *Referee:* Zsolt (Hungary)

26.6.54 **Italy** (1) **4 Belgium** (0) 1 *Lugano*

Italy: Ghezzi; Magnini, Giacomazzi, Neri, Tognon, Nesti, Frignani (1), Cappello, Galli (1), Pandolfini (pen.), Lorenzi (1)
Belgium: Gernaey; Dries, Van Brandt, Huysmans, Carre, Mees, Mermans, Van den Bosch H., Coppens, Anoul (1), Van den Bosch P.
Referee: Steiner (Austria)

	P	W	D	L	F	A	Pts
England	2	1	1	0	6	4	3
Switzerland	2	1	0	1	2	3	2
Italy	2	1	0	1	5	3	2
Belgium	2	0	1	1	5	8	1

PLAY-OFF FOR 2nd PLACE

23.6.54 **Switzerland** (1) **4 Italy** (0) 1 *Basle*

Switzerland: Parlier; Neury, Kernen, Eggimann, Bocquet, Casali, Antenen, Vonlanthen, Hugi II (2), Ballaman (1), Fatton (1)
Italy: Viola; Magnini, Giacomazzi, Mari, Tognon, Nesti (1), Muccinelli, Pandolfini, Lorenzi, Segato, Frignani *Referee:* Griffiths (Wales)

QUARTER-FINALS

26.6.54 **Austria** (5) 7 **Switzerland** (4) 5 *Lausanne*

Austria: as 19.6.54, Hanappi (o.g.), Ocwirk (1), Wagner (3), Probst (1), Korner A. (2)
Switzerland: as 23.6.54, Hugi II (2), Ballaman (2)

Referee: Faultless (Scotland)

26.6.54 **Uruguay** (2) **4 England** (1) 2 *Basle*

Uruguay: as 16.6.54, Varela (1), Ambrois (1), Borges (1), Schiaffino (1)
England: Merrick; Staniforth, Byrne, McGarry, Wright, Dickinson, Matthews, Broadis, Lofthouse (1), Wilshaw, Finney (1)
Referee: Steiner (Austria)

27.6.54 **West Germany** (1) 2 **Yugoslavia** (0) 0 *Geneva*

West Germany: Turek; Laband, Kohlmeyer, Eckel, Liebrich, Mai, Rahn (1), Morlock, Walter O., Walter F., Schafer
Yugoslavia: as 16.6.54, Horvat (o.g.) *Referee:* Zsolt (Hungary)

27.6.54 **Hungary** (2) **4 Brazil** (1) 2 *Berne*

Hungary: Grosics; Buzanszky, Lantos (pen.), Bozsik, Lorant, Zakarias, Toth M., Kocsis (2), Hidegkuti (1), Czibor, Toth J.
Brazil: Castilho; Santos D. (pen.), Santos N., Brandaozinho, Pinheiro, Bauer, Julinho (1), Didi, Indio, Humberto, Maurinho
Referee: Ellis (England)

Vava, Brazil, is the only player to have scored in successive World Cup finals, scoring twice in 1958 and once in 1962.

SEMI-FINALS

30.6.54 **West Germany** (1) 6 **Austria** (0) 1 *Basle*

West Germany: Turek; Posipal, Kohlmeyer, Eckel, Liebrich, Mai, Rahn, Morlock (1), Walter O. (2), Walter F. (2 pens.), Schafer (1)
Austria: Zeman; Hanappi, Schleger, Ocwirk, Happel, Koller, Korner R., Wagner, Stojaspal, Probst (1), Korner A. *Referee:* Orlandini (Italy)

30.6.54 **Hungary** (1) **4 Uruguay** (0) 2 (2-2 at 90 mins) *Lausanne*

Hungary: Grosics; Buzanszky, Lantos, Bozsik, Lorant, Zakarias, Budai, Kocsis (2), Palotas, Hidegkuti (1), Czibor (1)
Uruguay: Maspoli; Santamaria, Martinez, Andrade, Carballo, Cruz, Souto, Ambrois, Schiaffino, Hohberg (2), Borges *Referee:* Griffiths (Wales)

MATCH FOR THIRD PLACE

3.7.54 **Austria** (1) 3 **Uruguay** (1) 1 *Zurich*

Austria: Schmied; Hanappi, Barschandt, Ocwirk (1), Kollmann, Koller, Korner R., Wagner, Dienst, Stojaspal (pen.), Probst
Uruguay: Maspoli; Santamaria, Martinez, Andrade, Carballo, Cruz (o.g.), Abbadie, Hohberg (1), Mendez, Schiaffino, Borges
Referee: Wyssling (Switzerland)

FINAL

4.7.54 **West Germany** (2) 3 **Hungary** (2) 2 *Berne* Attendance: 60,000

West Germany: as semi-final, Rahn (2), Morlock (1)
Hungary: Grosics; Buzanszky, Lantos, Bozsik, Lorant, Zakarias, Czibor (1), Kocsis, Hidegkuti, Puskas (1), Toth J. *Referee:* Ling (England)

West Germany achieved the highest scoring rate for a winning World Cup side when in 1954 they scored 25 goals in 6 matches for an average of 4.16 per game. But the 14 goals they conceded was also a record.

1958

Though England, Northern Ireland, Scotland and Wales all reached the finals in Sweden it was George Raynor, the English-born manager of the host nation who almost achieved the impossible with a team packed with ageing exiles brought from Italy.

Against any country other than Brazil, who had been perfecting a 4-2-4 system, the Swedes might have succeeded. By stealing the ball, rather than tackling for it, and plundering opposing defences the Brazilians emerged as the first team to win the World Cup outside their own continent.

It was the most truly representative competition. 46 of the 53 original entries played in 89 qualifying games, watched by 4 million spectators.

For the first time no team other than host and holder had a bye to the finals, and when no opponent could be found for politically isolated Israel, Wales made the most of their second chance ballot success.

Though Scotland disappointed, Wales, Northern Ireland and England – despite the Munich air disaster the previous February in which they lost Roger Byrne, Duncan Edwards and Tommy Taylor – were not disgraced.

The French tandem of Just Fontaine (with 13 goals, the leading marksman) and Raymond Kopa impressed, but were overshadowed by a Brazilian trio: a teenage prodigy called Pele, a devastating right winger in Garrincha, and Didi, an inside-forward of rare delicacy.

1958 GROUP 1

8.6.58 **West Germany** (2) 3 **Argentina** (1) 1 *Malmo*

West Germany: Herkenrath; Stollenwerk, Juskowiak, Eckel, Erhardt, Szymaniak, Rahn (2), Walter F., Seeler (1), Schmidt, Schafer
Argentina: Carrizo; Dellacha, Vairo, Lombardo, Rossi, Varacka, Corbatta (1), Prado, Menendez, Rojas, Cruz *Referee:* Leafe (England)

8.6.58 **Northern Ireland** (1) 1 **Czechoslovakia** (0) 0 *Halmstad*

Northern Ireland: Gregg; Keith, McMichael, Blanchflower, Cunningham, Peacock, Bingham, Cush (1), Dougan, McIlroy, McParland
Czechoslovakia: Dolejsi; Mraz, Novak, Pluskal, Cadek, Masopust, Hovorka, Dvorak, Borovicka, Hertl, Krauss *Referee:* Seipelt (Austria)

11.6.58 **West Germany** (0) 2 **Czechoslovakia** (2) 2 *Halsingborg*

West Germany: Herkenrath; Stollenwerk, Juskowiak, Schnellinger, Erhardt, Szymaniak, Rahn (1), Walter F., Seeler, Schafer (1), Klodt
Czechoslovakia: Dolejsi; Mraz, Novak, Pluskal, Popluhar, Masopust, Hovorka, Dvorak (pen.), Molnar, Feureisl, Zikan (1)
Referee: Ellis (England)

11.6.58 **Argentina** (1) 3 **Northern Ireland** (1) 1 *Halmstad*

Argentina: Carrizo; Dellacha, Vairo, Lombardo, Rossi, Varacka, Corbatta (pen.), Avio (1), Menendez (1), Labruna, Boggio
Northern Ireland: Gregg; Keith, McMichael, Blanchflower, Cunningham, Peacock, Bingham, Cush, Coyle, McIlroy, McParland (1)
Referee: Ahlner (Sweden)

15.6.58 **West Germany** (1) 2 **Northern Ireland** (1) 2 *Malmo*

West Germany: Herkenrath; Stollenwerk, Juskowiak, Eckel, Erhardt, Szymaniak, Rahn (1), Walker F., Seeler (1), Schafer, Klodt
Northern Ireland: Gregg; Keith, McMichael, Blanchflower, Cunningham, Peacock, Bingham, Cush, Casey, McIlroy, McParland (2)
Referee: Campos (Portugal)

15.6.58 **Czechoslovakia** (3) 6 **Argentina** (0) 1 *Halsingborg*

Czechoslovakia: Dolejsi; Mraz, Novak, Dvorak (1), Popluhar, Masopust, Hovorka (1), Borovicka, Molnar, Feureisl (2), Zikan (2)
Argentina: Carrizo; Dellacha, Vairo, Lombardo, Rossi, Varacka, Corbatta (1), Avio, Menendez, Labruna, Cruz *Referee:* Ellis (England)

	P	W	D	L	F	A	Pts
West Germany	3	1	2	0	7	5	4
Northern Ireland	3	1	1	1	4	5	3
Czechoslovakia	3	1	1	1	8	4	3
Argentina	3	1	0	2	5	10	2

PLAY-OFF FOR 2nd PLACE

17.6.58 **Northern Ireland** (1) 2 **Czechoslovakia** (1) 1 *Malmo*
(after extra time; 1-1 at 90 mins)

Northern Ireland: Uprichard; Keith, McMichael, Blanchflower, Cunningham, Peacock, Bingham, Cush, Scott, McIlroy, McParland (2)
Czechoslovakia: Dolejsi; Mraz, Novak, Bubernik, Popluhar, Masopust, Dvorak, Molnar, Feureisl, Borovicka, Zikan (1) *Referee:* Guigue (France)

GROUP 2

8.6.58 **Yugoslavia** (1) 1 **Scotland** (0) 1 *Vasteras*

Yugoslavia: Beara; Sijakovic, Crnkovic, Krstic, Zebec, Boskov, Petakovic (1), Veselinovic, Milutinovic, Sekularac, Rajkov
Scotland: Younger; Caldow, Hewie, Turnbull, Evans, Cowie, Leggat, Murray (1), Mudie, Collins, Imlach *Referee:* Wyssling (Switzerland)

8.6.58 **France** (2) 7 **Paraguay** (2) 3 *Norrkoping*

France: Remetter; Kaelbel, Lerond, Penverne, Jonquet, Marcel, Wisnieski (1), Fontaine (3), Kopa (1), Piantoni (1), Vincent (1)
Paraguay: Mageregger; Miranda, Arevalo, Villalba, Lezcano, Achucarro, Aguero, Parodi, Romero (1), Re, Amarilla (2, 1 pen.)
Referee: Gardeazabal (Spain)

11.6.58 **Paraguay** (2) 3 **Scotland** (1) 2 *Norrkoping*

Paraguay: Aguilar; Arevalo, Echague, Villalba, Lezcano, Achucarro, Aguero (1), Parodi, Romero (1), Re (1), Amarilla
Scotland: Younger; Parker, Caldow, Turnbull, Evans, Cowie, Leggat, Collins (1), Mudie (1), Robertson, Fernie *Referee:* Orlandini (Italy)

11.6.58 **Yugoslavia** (1) 3 **France** (1) 2 *Vasteras*

Yugoslavia: Beara; Tomic, Crnkovic, Krstic, Zebec, Boskov, Petakovic (1), Veselinovic (2), Milutinovic, Sekularac, Rajkov
France: Remetter; Kaelbel, Marche, Penverne, Jonquet, Lerond, Wisnieski, Fontaine (2), Kopa, Piantoni, Vincent *Referee:* Griffiths (Wales)

15.6.58 **France** (2) 2 **Scotland** (0) 1 *Orebro*

France: Abbes; Kaelbel, Lerond, Penverne, Jonquet, Marcel, Wisnieski, Fontaine (1), Kopa (1), Piantoni, Vincent
Scotland: Brown; Caldow, Hewie, Turnbull, Evans, Mackay, Collins, Murray, Mudie, Baird (1), Imlach *Referee:* Brozzi (Argentina)

Just Fontaine, France, scored in every match in 1958 and his 13 goals is an unbeaten record by a player in one final competition.

15.6.58 **Paraguay** (1) 3 **Yugoslavia** (2) 3 *Eskilstuna*

Paraguay: as 11.6.58, Aguero (1), Parodi (1), Romero (1)
Yugoslavia: Beara; Tomic, Crnkovic, Krstic, Zebec, Boskov, Petakovic, Veselinovic (1), Ogjanovic (2), Sekularac, Rajkov
Referee: Macko (Czechoslovakia)

	P	W	D	L	F	A	Pts
France	3	2	0	1	11	7	4
Yugoslavia	3	1	2	0	7	6	4
Paraguay	3	1	1	1	9	12	3
Scotland	3	0	1	2	4	6	1

GROUP 3

8.6.58 **Sweden** (1) 3 **Mexico** (0) 0 *Stockholm*

Sweden: Svensson; Bergmark, Axbom, Liedholm (pen.), Gustavsson, Parling, Hamrin, Mellberg, Simonsson (2), Gren, Skoglund
Mexico: Carbajal; Del Muro, Villegas, Portugal, Romo, Flores, Hernandez, Reyes, Calderon, Gutierrez, Sesma *Referee:* Latyschev (USSR)

8.6.58 **Hungary** (1) 1 **Wales** (1) 1 *Sandviken*

Hungary: Grosics; Matrai, Sarosi, Bozsik (1), Sipos, Berendi, Sandor, Hidegkuti, Tichy, Bundzsak, Fenyvesi
Wales: Kelsey; Williams, Hopkins, Sullivan, Charles M., Bowen, Webster, Medwin, Charles J. (1), Allchurch, Jones *Referee:* Codesal (Uruguay)

11.6.58 **Mexico** (0) 1 **Wales** (1) 1 *Stockholm*

Mexico: Carbajal; Del Muro, Gutierrez, Cardenas, Romo, Flores, Belmonte (1), Reyes, Blanco, Gonzalez, Sesma
Wales: Kelsey; Williams, Hopkins, Baker, Charles M., Bowen, Webster, Medwin, Charles J., Allchurch (1), Jones *Referee:* Lemesic (Yugoslavia)

12.6.58 **Sweden** (2) 2 **Hungary** (0) 1 *Stockholm*

Sweden: as 8.6.58, Hamrin (2)
Hungary: Grosics; Matrai, Sarosi, Szojka, Sipos, Berendi, Sandor, Bundzsak, Bozsik, Tichy (1), Fenyvesi *Referee:* Mowat (Scotland)

15.6.58 **Sweden** (0) 0 **Wales** (0) 0 *Stockholm*

Sweden: Svensson; Bergmark, Axbom, Borjesson, Gustavsson, Parling, Berndtsson, Selmosson, Kallgren, Lofgren, Skoglund
Wales: Kelsey; Williams, Hopkins, Sullivan, Charles M., Bowen, Vernon, Hewitt, Charles J., Allchurch, Jones *Referee:* Van Nuffel (Belgium)

15.6.58 **Hungary** (1) 4 **Mexico** (0) 0 *Sandviken*

Hungary: Ilku; Matrai, Sarosi, Szojka, Sipos, Kotasz, Budai, Bencsics, Hidegkuti, Tichy (2), Sandor (1)
Mexico: Carbajal; Del Muro, Gutierrez, Cardenas, Sepulveda, Flores, Belmonte, Reyes, Blanco, Gonzalez (o.g.), Sesma
Referee: Eriksson (Finland)

	P	W	D	L	F	A	Pts
Sweden	3	2	1	0	5	1	5
Wales	3	0	3	0	2	2	3
Hungary	3	1	1	1	6	3	3
Mexico	3	0	1	2	1	8	1

PLAY-OFF FOR 2nd PLACE

17.6.58 **Wales** (0) 2 **Hungary** (1) 1 *Stockholm*

Wales: Kelsey; Williams, Hopkins, Sullivan, Charles M., Bowen, Medwin (1), Hewitt, Charles J., Allchurch (1), Jones
Hungary: Grosics; Matrai, Sarosi, Bozsik, Sipos, Kostasz, Budai, Bencsics, Tichy (1), Bundzsak, Fenyvesi *Referee:* Latyschev (USSR)

GROUP 4

8.6.58 **USSR** (1) 2 **England** (0) 2 *Gothenburg*

USSR: Yashin; Kessarov, Kusnezov, Voinov, Krischevsky, Zarev, Ivanov A., Ivanov V. (1), Simonian (1), Salnikov, Iljin
England: McDonald; Howe, Banks, Clamp, Wright, Slater, Douglas, Robson, Kevan (1), Haynes, Finney (pen.) *Referee:* Zsolt (Hungary)

8.6.58 **Brazil** (1) 3 **Austria** (0) 0 *Udevalla*

Brazil: Gylmar; De Sordi, Santos N. (1), Dino, Bellini, Orlando, Joel, Didi, Mazzola (2), Dida, Zagalo
Austria: Szanwald; Halla, Svoboda, Hanappi, Happel, Koller, Horak, Senekowitsch, Buzek, Korner A., Schleger *Referee:* Guigue (France)

11.6.58 **Brazil** (0) 0 **England** (0) 0 *Gothenburg*

Brazil: Gylmar; De Sordi, Santos N., Dino, Bellini, Orlando, Joel, Didi, Mazzola, Vava, Zagalo
England: McDonald; Howe, Banks, Clamp, Wright, Slater, Douglas, Robson, Kevan, Haynes, A'Court *Referee:* Dusch (West Germany)

11.6.58 **USSR** (1) 2 **Austria** (0) 0 *Boras*

USSR: as 8.6.58, Ivanov V. (1), Iljin (1)
Austria: Schmied; Kozliczek E., Svoboda, Hanappi, tstotz, Koller, Horak, Kozliczek P., Buzek, Korner A., Senekowitsch
Referee: Jorgensen (Denmark)

15.6.58 **Brazil** (1) 2 **USSR** (0) 0 *Gothenburg*

Brazil: Gylmar; De Sordi, Santos N., Zito, Bellini, Orlando, Garrincha, Didi, Vava (2), Pele, Zagalo
USSR: Yashin; Kessarov, Kusnezov, Voinov, Krischevsky, Zarev, Ivanov A., Ivanov V., Simonjan, Netto, Iljin *Referee:* Guigue (France)

15.6.58 **England** (0) 2 **Austria** (1) 2 *Boras*

England: as 11.6.58, Kevan (1), Haynes (1)
Austria: Szanwald; Kollmann, Svoboda, Hanappi, Happel, Koller (1), Kozliczek E., Kozliczek P., Buzek, Korner A. (1), Senekowitsch
Referee: Asmussen (Denmark)

	P	W	D	L	F	A	Pts
Brazil	3	2	1	0	5	0	5
USSR	3	1	1	1	4	4	3
England	3	0	3	0	4	4	3
Austria	3	0	1	2	2	7	1

The two players with the shortest names to have appeared in a World Cup final tournament are Cavetano Re (Paraguay) in 1958 and Francisco Sa (Argentina) in 1974.

PLAY-OFF FOR 2nd PLACE

17.6.58 **USSR** (0) 1 **England** (0) 0 *Gothenburg*

USSR: Yashin; Kessarov, Kusnezov, Voinov, Krischevsky, Zarev, Apuchtin, Ivanov V., Simonian, Falin, Iljin (1)
England: McDonald; Howe, Banks, Clayton, Wright, Slater, Brabrook, Broadbent, Kevan, Haynes, A'Court *Referee:* Dusch (West Germany)

QUARTER-FINALS

19.6.58 **West Germany** (1) 1 **Yugoslavia** (0) 0 *Malmo*

West Germany: as 8.6.58, Rahn (1)
Yugoslavia: Krivokuca; Sijakovic, Crnkovic, Boskov, Zebec, Krstic, Petakovic, Ogjanovic, Milutinovic, Veselinovic, Rajkov
Referee: Wyssling (Switzerland)

19.6.58 **France** (1) **4 Northern Ireland** (0) 0 *Norrkoping*

France: as 15.6.58, Fontaine (2), Wisnieski (1), Piantoni (1)
Northern Ireland: Gregg; Keith, McMichael, Blanchflower, Cunningham, Cush, Bingham, Casey, Scott, McIlroy, McParland
Referee: Gardeazabal (Spain)

19.6.58 **Sweden** (0) 2 **USSR** (0) 0 *Stockholm*

Sweden: Svensson; Bergmark, Axbom, Borjesson, Gustavsson, Parling, Hamrin (1), Gren, Simonsson (1), Liedholm, Skoglund
USSR: as 8.6.58 *Referee:* Leafe (England)

19.6.58 **Brazil** (0) 1 **Wales** (0) 0 *Gothenburg*

Brazil: Gylmar, De Sordi, Santos N., Zito, Bellini, Orlando, Garrincha, Didi, Mazzola, Pele (1), Zagalo
Wales: Kelsey; Williams, Hopkins, Sullivan, Charles M., Bowen, Medwin, Hewitt, Webster, Allchurch, Jones *Referee:* Seipelt (Austria)

Uwe Seeler, West Germany, holds the record for appearances in World Cup final tournaments. He appeared in 21 matches during the 1958, 1962, 1966 and 1970 series, scoring nine goals.

SEMI-FINALS

24.6.58 **Sweden** (1) 3 **West Germany** (1) 1 *Gothenburg*

Sweden: as quarter-finals, Hamrin (1), Gren (1), Skoglund (1)
West Germany: Herkenrath; Stollenwerk, Eckel, Erhardt, Szymaniak, Juskowiak, Rahn, Walter F., Seeler, Schafer (1), Cieslarczyk
Referee: Zsolt (Hungary)

24.6.58 **Brazil** (2) 5 **France** (1) 2 *Stockholm*

Brazil: as 15.6.58, Pele (3), Vava (1), Didi (1)
France: as quarter-finals, Fontaine (1), Piantoni (1) *Referee:* Griffiths (Wales)

MATCH FOR THIRD PLACE

28.6.58 **France** (3) 6 **West Germany** (1) 3 *Gothenburg*

France: Abbes; Kaelbel, Lerond, Penverne, Lafond, Marcel, Wisnieski, Douis (1), Kopa (pen.), Fontaine (4), Vincent
West Germany: Kwiatkowski; Stollenwerk, Erhardt, Schnellinger, Wewers, Szymaniak, Rahn (1), Sturm, Kelbassa, Schafer (1), Cieslarczyk (1)
Referee: Brozzi (Argentina)

FINAL

29.6.58 **Brazil** (2) 5 **Sweden** (1) 2 *Stockholm* Attendance: 49,737

Brazil: Gylmar; Santos D., Santos N., Zito, Bellini, Orlando, Garrincha, Didi, Vava (2), Pele (2), Zagalo (1)
Sweden: as semi and quarter-finals, Simonsson (1), Liedholm (1)
Referee: Guigue (France)

1962

In the Battle of Santiago, the blackspot of the competition, Chile's outside-left Leonel Sanchez, son of a professional boxer, broke the nose of the Italian Humberto Maschio with a flawless left hook clearly seen by television and film audiences, but missed by the two linesmen and referee.

Not so fortunate was Italian defender Mario David whose retaliatory kick aimed at Sanchez ended in dismissal, though years afterwards Sanchez admitted that David had not touched him.

While the Italians had failed to stamp the right kind of authority on the matches themselves, their *catenaccio* defensive system was to lead others to negative play. Goalscoring rates dropped alarmingly. Even the Brazilians, who beat Czechoslovakia in the final, were more cautious and pulled winger Mario Zagalo into midfield for a 4-3-3-strategy.

England as the only home country to qualify had succumbed to Brazil after reaching the quarter-finals, and Chile surprised their critics by finishing third.

4 venues were utilised: a new stadium in Santiago had been finished in December, another more modest ground was located at the coastal town of Vina del Mar, while Rancagua and Arica completed the sites.

1962 GROUP 1

30.5.62 **Uruguay** (0) 2 **Colombia** (1) 1 *Arica*

Uruguay: Sosa; Troche, Alvarez E. W., Mendez, Goncalvez, Alvarez E., Cubilla (1), Rocha, Langon, Sasia (1), Perez
Colombia: Sanchez C; Gonzalez J., Lopez, Echeverri, Zuluaga (1), Silva, Aceros, Coll, Klinger, Gamboa, Arias *Referee:* Dorogi (Hungary)

31.5.62 **USSR** (0) 2 **Yugoslavia** (0) 0 *Arica*

USSR: Yashin; Dubinski, Maslonkin, Ostrovsky, Voronin, Netto, Metreveli, Ivanov V. (1), Ponedelnik (1), Kanevski, Meschki
Yugoslavia: Soskic; Durkovic, Jusufi, Matus, Markovic, Popovic, Mujic, Sekularac, Kerkovic, Galic, Skoblar *Referee:* Dusch (West Germany)

2.6.62 **Yugoslavia** (2) 3 **Uruguay** (1) 1 *Arica*

Yugoslavia: Soskic; Durkovic, Radakovic, Markovic, Jusufi, Popovic, Melic, Sekularac, Jerkovic (1), Galic (1), Skoblar (1)
Uruguay: Sosa; Troche, Alvarez E. W., Mendez, Goncalvez, Alvarez E., Rocha, Bergara, Cabrera (1), Sasia, Perez *Referee:* Galba (Czechoslovakia)

3.6.62 **USSR** (3) **4 Colombia** (1) **4** *Arica*

USSR: Yashin; Tschokeli, tostrovsky, Voronin, Maslonkin, Netto, Chislenko (1), Ivanov V. (2), Ponedelnik (1), Kanevski, Meschki
Colombia: Sanchez C; Alzate, Gonzalez J., Echeverri, Lopez, Serrano, Aceros (1), Coll (1), Klinger (1), Rada (1), Gonzalez H.
Referee: Filho (Brazil)

6.6.62 **USSR** (1) 2 **Uruguay** (0) 1 *Arica*

USSR: Yashin; Tschokeli, Voronin, Netto, Ostrovsky, Maslonkin, Chislenko, Ivanov V. (1), Ponedelnik, Mamykin (1), Chusainov
Uruguay: Sosa; Mendez, Alvarez E. W., Goncalvez, Alvarez E., Troche, Cubilla, Cortes, Cabrera, Sasia (1), Perez *Referee:* Jonni (Italy)

7.6.62 **Yugoslavia** (2) 5 **Colombia** (0) 0 *Arica*

Yugoslavia: Soskic; Durkovic, Jusufi, Radakovic, Markovic, Popovic, Ankovic, Sekularac, Jerkovic (3), Galic (1), Melic (1)
Colombia: as 3.6.62 *Referee:* Robles (Chile)

	P	W	D	L	F	A	Pts
USSR	3	2	1	0	8	5	5
Yugoslavia	3	2	0	1	8	3	4
Uruguay	3	1	0	2	4	6	2
Colombia	3	0	1	2	5	11	1

GROUP 2

30.5.62 **Chile** (1) 3 **Switzerland** (1) 1 *Santiago*

Chile: Escuti; Eyzaguirre, Sanchez R., Navarro, Contreras, Rojas, Ramirez (1), Toro, Landa, Fouilloux, Sanchez L. (2)
Switzerland: Elsener; Grobety, Morf, Weber, Schneiter, Tacchella, Antenen, Allemann, Wuthrich (1), Eschmann, Pottier *Referee:* Aston (England)

31.5.62 **West Germany** (0) 0 **Italy** (0) 0 *Santiago*

West Germany: Fahrian; Nowak, Schnellinger, Schulz, Erhardt, Szymaniak, Sturm, Haller, Seeler, Brulls, Schafer
Italy: Buffon; Losi, Robotti, Salvadore, Maldini, Radice, Ferrini, Rivera, Altafini, Sivori, Menichelli *Referee:* Davidson (Scotland)

2.6.62 **Chile** (0) 2 **Italy** (0) 0 *Santiago*

Chile: as 30.5.62, Ramirez (1), Toro (1)
Italy: Mattrel; David, Robotti, Salvadore, Janich, Tumburus, Mora, Maschio, Altafini, Ferrini, Menichelli *Referee:* Aston (England)

3.6.62 **West Germany** (1) 2 **Switzerland** (0) 1 *Santiago*

West Germany: Fahrian; Nowak, Schnellinger, Schulz, Erhardt, Szymaniak, Koslowski, Haller, Seeler (1), Schafer, Brulls (1)
Switzerland: Elsener; Schneiter (1), Tacchella, Grobety, Wuthrich, Weber, Antenen, Vonlanthen, Eschmann, Allemann, Durr
Referee: Horn (Netherlands)

6.6.62 **West Germany** (1) 2 **Chile** (0) 0 *Santiago*

West Germany: Fahrian; Nowak, Schnellinger, Schulz, Ehardt, Giesemann, Kraus, Szymaniak (pen.), Seeler (1), Schafer, Brulls
Chile: Escuti; Eyzaguirre, Navarro, Contreras,Sanchez R., Rojas, Moreno, Tobar, Landa, Sanchez L., Ramirez *Referee:* Davidson (Scotland)

7.6.62 **Italy** (1) 3 **Switzerland** (0) 0 *Santiago*

Italy: Buffon; Losi, Radice, Salvadore, Maldini, Robotti, Mora (1), Bulgarelli (1), Sormani, Sivori, Pascutti (1)
Switzerland: Elsener; Schneiter, Tacchella, Grobety, Meier, Weber, Antenen, Vonlanthen, Wuthrich, Allemann, Durr *Referee:* Latyschev (USSR)

	P	**W**	**D**	**L**	**F**	**A**	**Pts**
West Germany	3	2	1	0	4	1	5
Chile	3	2	0	1	5	3	4
Italy	3	1	1	1	3	2	3
Switzerland	3	0	0	3	2	8	0

GROUP 3

30.5.62 **Brazil** (0) 2 **Mexico** (0) 0 *Vina del Mar*

Brazil: Gylmar; Santos D., Santos N., Zito, Mauro, Zozimo, Garrincha, Didi, Vava, Pele (1), Zagalo (1)
Mexico: Carbajal; Del Muro, Villegas, Cardenas, Sepulveda, Najera, Del Aguila, Reyes, Hernandez H., Jasso, Diaz *Referee:* Dienst (Switzerland)

Pele, Brazil, is the only player to have been with 3 World Cup winning teams, though through injury he missed the actual 1962 Final. He made 4 appearances in 1958, 2 in 1962 and 6 in 1970. He also played in 2 games in 1966. In these 14 appearances he scored 12 goals.

31.5.62 **Czechoslovakia** (0) 1 **Spain** (0) 0 *Vina del Mar*

Czechoslovakia: Schroif; Lala, Novak, Pluskal, Popluhar, Masopust, Stibranyi (1), Scherer, Kvasnak, Adamec, Jelinek
Spain: Carmelo; Rivilla, Reija, Segarra, Santamaria, Garay, Del Sol, Puskas, Martinez, Suarez, Gento *Referee:* Steiner (Austria)

2.6.62 **Brazil** (0) 0 **Czechoslovakia** (0) 0 Vina del Mar

Brazil: as 30.5.82
Czechoslovakia: as 31.5 62 *Referee:* Schwinte (France)

3.6.62 **Spain** (0) 1 **Mexico** (0) 0 *Vina del Mar*

Spain: Carmelo; Rodriguez, Gracia, Verges, Santamaria, Pachin, Del Sol, Peiro (1), Puskas, Suarez, Gento
Mexico: Carbajal; Del Muro, Juaregui, Cardenas, Sepulveda, Jasso, Najera, Del Aguila, Reyes, Hernandez H., Diaz *Referee:* Tesanic (Yugoslavia)

6.6.62 **Brazil** (0) 2 **Spain** (1) 1 *Vina del Mar*

Brazil: Gylmar; Santos D., Santos N., Zito, Mauro, Zozimo, Garrincha, Didi, Vava, Amarildo (2), Zagalo
Spain: Araquistain; Rodriguez, Gracia, Verges, Echeverria, Pachin, Collar, Adelardo (1), Puskas, Peiro, Gento *Referee:* Bustamante (Chile)

7.6.62 **Mexico** (2) 3 **Czechoslovakia** (1) 1 *Vina del Mar*

Mexico: Carbajal; Del Muro, Sepulveda, Juaregui, Cardenas, Najera, Del Aguila (1), Hernandez A., Hernandez H. (pen.), Reyes, Diaz (1)
Czechoslovakia: Schroif; Lala, Novak, Pluskal, Popluhar, Masopust, Stibranyi, Scherer, Kvasnak, Adamec, Masek (1)
Referee: Dienst (Switzerland)

	P	W	D	L	F	A	Pts
Brazil	3	2	1	0	4	1	5
Czechoslovakia	3	1	1	1	2	3	3
Mexico	3	1	0	2	3	4	2
Spain	3	1	0	2	2	3	2

GROUP 4

30.5.62 **Argentina** (1) 1 **Bulgaria** (0) 0 *Rancagua*

Argentina: Roma; Navarro, Marzolini, Sainz, Sacchi, Paez, Facundo (1), Rossi, Pagani, Sanfilippo, Belen
Bulgaria: Naidenov; Rakarov, Dimitrov, Kitov, Kostov D., Kovatchev, Diev, Velitschkov, Iljev, Yakimov, Kolev *Referee:* Gardeazabal (Spain)

31.5.62 **Hungary** (1) 2 **England** (0) 1 *Rancagua*

Hungary: Grosics; Matrai, Meszoly, Sarosi, Solymosi, Sipos, Sandor, Rakosi, Tichy (1), Albert (1), Fenyvesi
England: Springett; Armfield, Wilson, Moore, Norman, Flowers (pen.), Douglas, Greaves, Hitchens, Haynes, Charlton R.
Referee: Horn (Netherlands)

2.6.62 **England** (2) 3 **Argentina** (0) 1 *Rancagua*

England: Springett; Armfield, Wilson, Moore, Norman, Flowers (pen.), Douglas, Greaves (1), Peacock, Haynes, Charlton R. (1)
Argentina: Roma; Cap, Marzolini, Sacchi, Navarro, Paez, Oleniak, Rattin, Sosa, Sanfilippo (1), Belen *Referee:* Latyschev (USSR)

3.6.62 **Hungary (4)** 6 **Bulgaria** (0) 1 *Rancagua*

Hungary: Ilku; Matrai, Sarosi, Solymosi (1), Meszoly, Sipos, Sandor, Gorocs, Albert (3), Tichy (2), Fenyvesi
Bulgaria: Naidenov; Rakarov, Kitov, Kostov D., Dimitrov, Kovatchev, Sokolov (1), Velitschkov, Asparoukhov, Kolev, Dermendjiev
Referee: Gardeazabal (Spain)

6.6.62 **Hungary** (0) 0 **Argentina** (0) 0 *Rancagua*

Hungary: Grosics;Matrai, Sarosi, Solymosi, Meszoly, Sipos, Kuharszky, Gorocs, Monostori, Tichy, Rakosi
Argentina: Dominguez; Sainz, Marzolini, Delgado, Cap, Sacchi, Facundo, Pando, Pagani, Oleniak, Gonzalez *Referee:* Yakasaki (Peru)

7.6.62 **England** (0) 0 **Bulgaria** (0) 0 *Rancagua*

England: Springett; Armfield, Wilson, Moore, Norman, Flowers, Douglas, Greaves, Peacock, Haynes, Charlton R.
Bulgaria: Naidenov; Pentshev, Jetchev, Kostov D., Dimitrov, Kovatchev, Kostov A., Velitschkov, Sokolov, Kolev, Dermendjiev
Referee: Blavier (Belgium)

	P	W	D	L	F	A	Pts
Hungary	3	2	1	0	8	2	5
England	3	1	1	1	4	3	3
Argentina	3	1	1	1	2	3	3
Bulgaria	3	0	1	2	1	7	1

QUARTER-FINALS

10.6.62 **Yugoslavia** (0) 1 **West Germany** (0) 0 *Santiago*

Yugoslavia: Soskic; Durkovic, Jusufi, Radakovic (1), Markovic, Popovic, Kovacevic, Sekularac, Jerkovic, Galic, Skoblar
West Germany: Fahrian; Nowak, Schnellinger, Schulz, Erhardt, Giesemann, Brulls, Haller, Seeler, Szymaniak, Schafer *Referee:* Yamasaki (Peru)

10.6.62 **Chile** (2) 2 **USSR** (1) 1 *Arica*

Chile: Escuti; Eyzaguirre, Navarro, Contreras, Sanchez R., Rojas (1), Ramirez, Toro, Landa, Tobar, Sanchez L. (1)
USSR: Yashin; Tschokeli, Ostrovsky, Voronin, Maslonkin, Netto, Chislenko (1), Ivanov V., Ponedelnik, Mamykin, Meschki
Referee: Horn (Netherlands)

10.6.62 **Brazil** (1) 3 **England** (1) 1 *Vina del Mar*

Brazil: as 6.6.62, Garrincha (2), Vava (1)
England: as 31.5.62, Hitchens (1) *Referee:* Schwinte (France)

10.6.62 **Czechoslovakia** (1) 1 **Hungary** (0) 0 *Rancagua*

Czechoslovakia: Schroif; Lala, Novak, Pluskal, Popluhar, Masopust, Pospichal, Scherer (1), Kadraba, Kvasnak, Jelinek
Hungary: as 31.5.62 *Referee:* Latyschev (USSR)

SEMI-FINALS

13.6.62 **Czechoslovakia** (0) 3 **Yugoslavia** (0) 1 *Vina del Mar*

Czechoslovakia: as quarter-finals, Scherer (2, 1 pen.), Kadraba (1)
Yugoslavia: Soskic; Durkovic, Jusufi, Radakovic, Markovic, Popovic, Sijakovic, Sekularac, Jerkovic (1), Galic, Skoblar
Referee: Dienst (Switzerland)

13.6.62 **Brazil** (2) **4 Chile** (1) 2 *Santiago*

Brazil: as quarter-finals, Garrincha (2), Vava (2)
Chile: Escuti; Eyzaguirre, Rodriguez, Contreras, Sanchez R., Rojas, Ramirez, Toro (1), Landa, Tobar, Sanchez L. (pen.) *Referee:* Yamasaki (Peru)

Brazil used only 12 players in the 1962 World Cup finals. Their one change came through injury to Pele who was replaced in later matches by Amarildo.

MATCH FOR THIRD PLACE

16.6.62 **Chile** (0) 1 **Yugoslavia** (0) 0 *Santiago*

Chile: Godoy; Eyzaguirre, Rodriguez, Cruz, Sanchez R., Rojas (1), Ramirez, Toro, Campos, Tobar, Sanchez L.
Yugoslavia: Soskic; Durkovic, Svinjarevic, Radakovic, Markovic, Popovic, Kovacevic, Sekularac, Jerkovic, Galic, Skoblar
Referee: Gardeazabal (Spain)

FINAL

17.6.62 **Brazil** (1) 3 **Czechoslovakia** (1) 1 *Santiago* Attendance: 68,679

Brazil: as semi- and quarter-finals, Zito (1), Vava (1), Amarildo (1)
Czechoslovakia: Schroif; Tichy. Novak, Pluskal, Popluhar, Masopust (1), Pospichal, Scherer, Kadraba, Kvasnak, Jelinek *Referee:* Latyschev (USSR)

Vava, Brazil, is the only player to have scored in successive World Cup finals, scoring twice in 1958 and once in 1962. Pele is the only other to have scored in two finals: twice in 1958 and once in 1970.

1966

Geoff Hurst became the only player to score a hat-trick in a World Cup final though there have probably never been three more controversial goals. The first was a header from a free-kick quickly taken while the referee was admonishing an opponent; the second hit the bar and came down so quickly that the referee consulted his Russian linesman, badly positioned 10 yards from the goal-line; the third came in the dying minutes with 3 spectators running down the opposite touchline.

That apart, Alf Ramsey's wingless Wembley wonders deserved their extra time win over the Germans who had prolonged their agony with a dramatic last minute equaliser.

In a tournament of cynical tackling, with players apparently fouling in rotation, 5 men were sent off: 2 Argentines, 2 Uruguayans and a Russian. 4 of the dismissals were against the often provocative West Germans, the other (Argentine captain Antonio Rattin) was sent off by a German referee for 'violence of the tongue' during a game against England.

North Korea surprised everyone with their carefree approach, humiliating Italy and at one point leading Portugal by 3 goals.

Financially it was another success. Final receipts alone were a record £200,000; total ticket sales £1.4 million. A television audience of 400 million was reached live through 33 world-wide networks, and film was despatched to a further 18.

1966 GROUP 1

11.7.66 **England** (0) 0 **Uruguay** (0) 0 *Wembley*

England: Banks; Cohen, Wilson, Stiles, Charlton J., Moore, Ball, Greaves, Hunt, Charlton R., Connelly
Uruguay: Mazurkiewicz; Troche, Manicera, Ubinas, Goncalvez, Caetano, Cortes, Viera, Silva, Rocha, Perez *Referee:* Zsolt (Hungary)

13.7.66 **France** (0) 1 **Mexico** (0) 1 *Wembley*

France: Aubour; Djorkaeff, Artelesa, Budzinski, De Michele, Bonnel, Bosquier, Combin, Herbin, Gondet, Hausser (1)
Mexico: Calderon; Chaires, Nunez, Hernandez, Pena, Mercado, Diaz, Reyes, Fragoso, Padilla, Borja (1) *Referee:* Ashkenasi (Israel)

15.7.66 **Uruguay** (2) 2 **France** (1) 1 *White City*

Uruguay: Mazurkiewicz; Troche, Manicera, Ubinas, Goncalvez, Caetano, Cortes (1), Viera, Sasia, Rocha (1), Perez
France: Aubour; Djorkaeff, Artelesa, Budzinski, Bosquier, Bonnel, Simon, Herbet, De Bourgoing (pen.), Gondet, Hausser
Referee: Galba (Czechoslovakia)

16.7.66 **England** (1) 2 **Mexico** (0) 0 *Wembley*

England: Banks; Cohen, Wilson, Stiles, Charlton J., Moore, Paine, Greaves, Hunt (1), Charlton R. (1), Peters
Mexico: Calderon; Chaires, Pena, Del Muro, Juaregui, Diaz, Padilla, Borja, Nunez, Reyes, Hernandez *Referee:* Lo Bello (Italy)

19.7.66 **Uruguay** (0) 0 **Mexico** (0) 0 *Wembley*

Uruguay: as 15.7.66
Mexico: Carbajal; Chaires, Pena, Nunez, Hernandez, Diaz, Mercado, Reyes, Cisneros, Borja, Padilla *Referee:* Loow (Sweden)

20.7.66 **England** (1) 2 **France** (0) 0 *Wembley*

England: Banks; Cohen, Wilson, Stiles, Charlton J., Moore, Callaghan, Greaves, Hunt (2), Charlton R., Peters
France: Aubour; Djorkaeff, Artelesa, Budzinski, Bosquier, Bonnel, Simon, Herbet, Gondet, Herbin, Hausser *Referee:* Yamasaki (Peru)

	P	W	D	L	F	A	Pts
England	3	2	1	0	4	0	5
Uruguay	3	1	2	0	2	1	4
Mexico	3	0	2	1	1	3	2
France	3	0	1	2	2	5	1

GROUP 2

12.7.66 **West Germany** (3) 5 **Switzerland** (0) 0 *Sheffield*

West Germany: Tilkowski; Hottges, Weber, Schulz, Schnellinger, Beckenbauer (2), Haller (2, 1 pen.), Brulls, Seeler, Overath, Held (1)
Switzerland: Elsener; Grobety, Schneiter, Tacchella, Fuhrer, Bani, Durr, Odermatt, Kunzli, Hosp, Schindelholz *Referee:* Phillips (Scotland)

13.7.66 **Argentina** (0) 2 **Spain** (0) 1 *Birmingham*

Argentina: Roma; Ferreiro, Perfumo, Albrecht, Marzolini, Solari, Rattin, Gonzalez, Artime (2), Onega, Mas
Spain: Iribar; Sanchis, Gallego, Zoco, Eladio, Pirri (1), Suarez, Del Sol, Ufarte, Peiro, Gento *Referee:* Rumentschev (Bulgaria)

15.7.66 **Spain** (0) 2 **Switzerland** (1) 1 *Sheffield*

Spain: Iribar; Sanchis (1), Gallego, Zoco, Reija, Pirri, Del Sol, Amancio (1), Peiro, Suarez, Gento
Switzerland: Elsener; Fuhrer, Brodmann, Leimgruber, Stierli, Bani, Armbruster, Gottardi, Hosp, Kuhn, Quentin (1)
Referee: Bakhramov (USSR)

16.7.66 **West Germany** (0) 0 **Argentina** (0) 0 *Birmingham*

West Germany: as 12.7.66.
Argentina: as 13.7.66. *Referee:* Zecevic (Yugoslavia)

19.7.66 **Argentina** (0) 2 **Switzerland** (0) 0 *Sheffield*

Argentina: Roma; Ferreiro, Perfumo, Calics, Marzolini, Solari, Rattin, Gonzalez, Artime (1), Onega (1), Mas
Switzerland: Eichmann; Fuhrer, Bani, Brodmann, Stierli, Armbruster, Kuhn, Gottardi, Kunzli, Hosp, Quentin *Referee:* Campos (Portugal)

20.7.66 **West Germany** (1) 2 **Spain** (1) 1 *Birmingham*

West Germany: Tilkowski; Hottges, Weber, Schulz, Schnellinger, Beckenbauer, Overath, Kramer, Seeler (1), Held, Emmerich (1)
Spain: Iribar; Sanchis, Gallego, Zoco, Reija, Glaria, Fuste (1), Amancio, Adelardo, Marcelino, Lapetra *Referee:* Marques (Brazil)

	P	**W**	**D**	**L**	**F**	**A**	**Pts**
West Germany	3	2	1	0	7	1	5
Argentina	3	2	1	0	4	1	5
Spain	3	1	0	2	4	5	2
Switzerland	3	0	0	3	1	9	0

GROUP 3

12.7.66 **Brazil** (1) 2 **Bulgaria** (0) 0 *Goodison Park*

Brazil: Gylmar; Santos D., Bellini, Altair, Paulo Henrique, Denilson, Lima, Garrincha (1), Alcindo, Pele (1), Jairzinho
Bulgaria: Naidenov; Chalamanov, Penev, Vutzov, Gaganelov, Kitov, Jetchev, Dermendjiev, Asparoukhov, Yakimov, Kolev
Referee: Tschenscher (West Germany)

13.7.66 **Portugal** (1) 3 **Hungary** (0) 1 *Old Trafford*

Portugal: Carvalho; Morais, Baptista, Vicente, Hilario, Graca, Coluna, Jose Augusto (2), Eusebio, Torres (1), Simoes
Hungary: Szentmihalyi; Kaposzta, Matrai, Meszoly, Sovari, Nagy I., Sipos, Bene (1), Albert, Farkas, Rakosi
Referee: Callaghan (Wales)

Brazil were unbeaten in 13 consecutive World Cup matches between 1958 and 1966, winning 11 and drawing 2. The run ended in a 3-1 defeat by Hungary.

15.7.66 **Hungary** (1) 3 **Brazil** (1) 1 *Goodison Park*

Hungary: Gelei; Matrai, Kaposzta, Meszoly (pen.), Sipos, Szepesi, Mathesz, Rakosi, Bene (1), Albert, Farkas (1)
Brazil: Gylmar; Santos D., Bellini, Altair, Paulo Henrique, Gerson, Lima, Garrincha, Alcindo, Tostao (1), Jairzinho *Referee:* Dagnall (England)

16.7.66 **Portugal** (2) 3 **Bulgaria** (0) 0 *Old Trafford*

Portugal: Pereira; Festa, Germano, Vicente, Hilario, Graca, Coluna, Jose Augusto, Eusebio (1), Torres (1), Simoes
Bulgaria: Naidenov; Chalamanov, Vutzov (o.g.), Gaganelov, Penev, Jetchev, Yakimov, Dermendjiev, Jekov, Asparoukhov, Kostov
Referee: Codesal (Uruguay)

19.7.66 **Portugal** (2) 3 **Brazil** (0) 1 *Goodison Park*

Portugal: Pereira; Morais, Baptista, Vicente, Hilario, Graca, Coluna, Jose Augusto, Eusebio (2), Torres, Simoes (1)
Brazil: Manga; Fidelis, Brito, Orlando, Rildo (1), Denilson, Lima, Jairzinho, Silva, Pele, Parana *Referee:* McCabe (England)

20.7.66 **Hungary** (2) 3 **Bulgaria** (1) 1 *Old Trafford*

Hungary: as 15.7.66, Meszoly (1), Bene (1)
Bulgaria: Simeonov; Penev, Largov, Vutzov, Gaganelov, Jetchev, Davidov (o.g.), Yakimov, Asparoukhov (1), Kolev, Kostov
Referee: Goicoechea (Argentina)

	P	**W**	**D**	**L**	**F**	**A**	**Pts**
Portugal	3	3	0	0	9	2	6
Hungary	3	2	0	1	7	5	4
Brazil	3	1	0	2	4	6	2
Bulgaria	3	0	0	3	1	8	0

GROUP 4

12.7.66 **USSR** (2) 3 **North Korea** (0) 0 *Ayresome Park*

USSR: Kavazashvili; Ponomarev, Shesternev, Khurtsilava, Ostrovsky, Sabo, Sichinava, Chislenko, Banischevski (1), Khusainov, Malofeyev (2)
North Korea: Chan Myung; Li Sup, Yung Kyoo, Bong Chil, Zoong Sun, Seung Hwi, Bong Zin, Doo Ik, Ryong Woon, Seung Il, Seung Zin
Referee: Gardeazabal (Spain)

13.7.66 **Italy** (1) 2 **Chile** (0) 0 *Roker Park*

Italy: Albertosi; Burgnich, Rosato, Salvadore, Facchetti, Bulgarelli, Lodetti, Perani, Mazzola (1), Rivera, Barison (1)
Chile: Olivares; Eyzaguirre, Cruz, Figueroa, Villanueva, Prieto, Marcos, Fouilloux, Araya, Tobar, Sanchez L. *Referee:* Dienst (Switzerland)

13.7.66 **North Korea** (0) 1 **Chile** (1) 1 *Ayresome Park*

North Korea: Chan Myung; Li Sup, Yung Kyoo, Zoong Sun, Yoon Kyung, Seung Zin (1), Seung Hwi, Bong Zin, Doo Ik, Dong Woon, Seung Il
Chile: Olivares; Valentini, Cruz, Figueroa, Villanueva, Prieto, Marcos (pen.), Araya, Landa, Fouilloux, Sanchez L.
Referee: Kandil (Egypt)

16.7.66 **USSR** (0) 1 **Italy** (0) 0 *Roker Park*

USSR: Yashin; Ponomarev, Shesternev, Khurtsilava, Danilov, Sabo, Voronin, Chislenko (1), Malofeyev, Banischevski, Khusainov
Italy: Albertosi; Burgnich, Rosato, Salvadore, Facchetti, Lodetti, Leoncini, Meroni, Mazzola, Bulgarelli, Pascutti *Referee:* Kreitlein (West Germany)

19.7.66 **North Korea** (1) 1 **Italy** (0) 0 *Ayresome Park*

North Korea: Chang Myung; Zoong Sun, Yung Kyoo, Yung Won, Yoon Kyung, Seung Hwi, Bong Zin, Doo Ik (1), Seung Zin, Bong Hwan, Seung Kook
Italy: Albertosi; Landini, Guarneri, Janich, Facchetti, Bulgarelli, Fogli, Perani, Mazzola, Rivera, Barison *Referee:* Schwinte (France)

20.7.66 **USSR** (1) 2 **Chile** (1) 1 *Roker Park*

USSR: Kavazashvili; Getmanov, Shesternev, Kornejev, Ostrovsky, Voronin, Afonin, Metreveli, Serebrannikov, Markarov, Porkujan (2)
Chile: Olivares; Valentini, Cruz, Figueroa, Villanueva, Marcos (1), Prieto, Araya, Landa, Yavar, Sanchez L. *Referee:* Adair (Northern Ireland)

	P	W	D	L	F	A	Pts
USSR	3	3	0	0	6	1	6
North Korea	3	1	1	1	2	4	3
Italy	3	1	0	2	2	2	2
Chile	3	0	1	2	2	5	1

QUARTER-FINALS

23.7.66 **England** (0) 1 **Argentina** (0) 0 *Wembley*

England: Banks; Cohen, Wilson, Stiles, Charlton J., Moore, Ball, Hunt, Hurst (1), Charlton R., Peters
Argentina: as 16.7.66 *Referee:* Kreitlein (West Germany)

23.7.66 **West Germany** (1) **4 Uruguay** (0) 0 *Sheffield*

West Germany: Tilkowski; Hottges, Weber, Schulz, Schnellinger, Haller (2), Beckenbauer (2), Overath, Seeler (1), Emmerich, Held
Uruguay: Mazurkiewicz; Troche, Ubinas, Caetano, Manicera, Rocha, Goncalvez, Salva, Cortes, Silva, Perez *Referee:* Finney (England)

23.7.66 **Portugal** (2) 5 **North Korea** (3) 3 *Goodison Park*

Portugal: as 19.7.66, Augusto (1), Eusebio (4, 2 pens.)
North Korea: Chan Myung; Zoong Sun, Yung Kyoo, Yung Won, Yoon Kyung, Seung Zin (1), Seung Hwi, Bong Zin, Doo Ik, Dong Woon (1), Seung Kook (1) *Referee:* Ashkenasi (Israel)

23.7.66 **USSR** (1) 2 **Hungary** (0) 1 *Roker Park*

USSR: Yashin; Ponomarev, Shesternev, Danilov, Voronin, Sabo, Khusainov, Chislenko (1), Banischevski, Malofeyev, Porkujan (1)
Hungary: Gelei; Kaposzta, Matrai, Meszoly, Szepesi, Nagy I., Sipos, Bene (1), Albert, Farkas, Rakosi *Referee:* Gardeazabal (Spain)

SEMI-FINALS

25.7.66 **West Germany** (1) 2 **USSR** (0) 1 *Goodison Park*

West Germany: Tilkowski; Lutz, Weber, Schulz, Schnellinger, Beckenbauer (1), Overath, Seeler, Haller (1), Held, Emmerich
USSR: as quarter-finals, Porkujan (1) *Referee:* Lo Bello (Italy)

26.7.66 **England** (1) 2 **Portugal** (0) 1 *Wembley*

England: as quarter-finals, Charlton R. (2)
Portugal: Pereira; Festa, Baptista, Jose Carlos, Hilario, Graca, Coluna, Jose Augusto, Eusebio (pen.), Torres, Simoes *Referee:* Schwinte (France)

MATCH FOR THIRD PLACE

28.7.66 **Portugal** (1) 2 **USSR** (1) 1 *Wembley*

Portugal: as semi-finals, Eusebio (pen.), Torres (1)
USSR: Yashin; Ponomarev, Korneev, Khurtsilava, Danilov, Voronin, Sichinava, Serebrannikov, Banischevski, Malofeyev (1), Metreveli
Referee: Dagnall (England)

FINAL

30.7.66 **England** (1) **4 West Germany** (1) 2 *Wembley* Attendance: 93,802
(after extra time; 2-2 at 90 mins)

England: as quarter- and semi-finals, Hurst (3), Peters (1)
West Germany: as quarter-finals, Weber (1), Haller (1)
Referee: Dienst (Switzerland)

Geoff Hurst, England, is the only player to have scored a hat-trick in a World Cup Final. He achieved three goals against West Germany in 1966 when England won 4-2.

1970

Brazil ably tackled the problems of altitude in Mexico during their meticulous four months preparation and were rewarded with a vintage victory in the final. They succeeded not only through this single-minded devotion to detail but because of several outstanding individuals and despite many defensive problems. Goalkeeper Felix was uncertain, their four man zonal defence exposing itself on the flanks and often giving him less than adequate cover. But, moving forward they were almost irresistible. Apart from their being restricted to a single goal by a plucky England side (who later lost by underestimating the Germans) Brazil scored freely with a versatile, flexible striking force.

There was the deceptively languid Gerson as midfield master, Tostao unselfish in attack despite a vulnerable eye injury, and Jairzinho their penetrating winger. There was the industry of Clodoaldo, the explosive dead ball shooting of Rivelino and above all the individual genius of Pele whose wide peripheral vision added an unmatched dimension to his play.

In contrast Italy reached the final having scored just once in their group and four times in a farcical, 7-goal extra time semi-final with West Germany. They were then well beaten by Brazil.

FIFA who had brought in the use of red and yellow cards at the Mexico Olympics used them effectively in the tournament; there was a rash of cautions, but no dismissals.

1970 GROUP 1

31.5.70 **Mexico** (0) 0 **USSR** (0) 0 *Mexico City*

Mexico: Calderon; Pena, Perez, Hernandez, Lopez, Vantolra, Guzman, Pulido, Velarde (Manguia), Valdivia, Fragoso
USSR: Kavazashvili; Kaplichny, Lovchev, Logofet, Shesternev, Asatiani, Muntian, Serebrannikov (Puzach), Nodia (Khmelnitzki), Byshovets, Evryushikhin *Referee:* Tschenscher (West Germany)

3.6.70 **Belgium** (1) 3 **El Salvador** (0) 0 *Mexico City*

Belgium: Piot; Heylens, Thissen, Dewalque, Dockx, Semmeling (Polleunis), Van Moer (2), Devrindt, Van Himst, Puis, Lambert (pen.)
El Salvador: Magana; Rivas, Mariona, Osorio, Quintanilla, Rodriguez Lindo (Sermeno), Vasquez, Martinez, Cabezas, Aparicio, Manzano (Mendes C.) *Referee:* Radulescu (Rumania)

6.6.70 **USSR** (1) **4 Belgium** (0) 1 *Mexico City*

USSR: Kavazashvili; Dzodzuashvili (Kiselev), Afonin, Shesternev, Khurtsilava, Kaplichny (Lovchev), Asatiani (1), Muntian, Byshovets (2), Evryushikhin, Khmelnitzki (1)
Belgium: Piot; Heylens, Thissen, Dewalque, Jeck, Dockx, Semmeling, Van Moer, Van Himst, Puis, Lambert (1) *Referee:* Scheurer (Switzerland)

7.6.70 **Mexico** (1) **4 El Salvador** (0) 0 *Mexico City*

Mexico: Calderon; Vantolra, Pena, Guzman, Perez, Gonzalez, Munguia, Valdivia (2), Borja (Lopez then Basaguren (1)), Fragoso (1), Padilla
El Salvador: Magana; Rivas, Mariona, Osorio, Mendez C. (Monge), Quintanilla, Rodriguez Lindo, Vasquez, Martinez, Cabezas, Aparicio (Mendez S.) *Referee:* Kandil (Egypt)

10.6.70 **USSR** (0) 2 **El Salvador** (0) 0 *Mexico City*

U SR: Kavazashvili; Dzodzuashvili, Khurtsilava, Shesternev, Afonin, Kiselev (Asatiani), Serebrannikov, Muntian, Pusach (Evryuzhikhin), Byshovets (2), Khmelnitzki
El Salvador: Magana; Rivas, Mariona, Castro, Osorio, Vasquez, Portillo, Cabezas (Aparicio), Rodriguez Lindo (Sermeno), Mendez S., Monge *Referee:* Hormazabal (Chile)

11.6.70 **Mexico** (1) 1 **Belgium** (0) 0 *Mexico City*

Mexico: Calderon; Vantolra, Guzman, Pena (pen.), Perez, Pulido, Gonzalez, Munguia, Padilla, Valdivia (Basaguren), Fragoso
Belgium: Piot; Heylens, Thissen, Dewalque, Jeck, Dockx, Semmeling, Van Moer, Van Himst, Puis, Polleunis (Devrindt) *Referee:* Coerezza (Argentina)

	P	W	D	L	F	A	Pts
USSR	3	2	1	0	6	1	5
Mexico	3	2	1	0	5	0	5
Belgium	3	1	0	2	4	5	2
El Salvador	3	0	0	3	0	9	0

GROUP 2

2.6.70 **Uruguay** (1) 2 **Israel** (0) 0 *Puebla*

Uruguay: Mazurkiewicz; Ubinas, Ancheta, Matosas, Mujica (1), Montero Castillo, Rocha (Cortes), Maneiro (1), Cubilla, Esparrago, Losado
Israel: Vissoker; Schwager, Rosen, Rosenthal, Primo, Spiegel, Shum, Spiegler, Talbi (Bar), Faygenbaum, Rom (Vollach)
Referee: Davidson (Scotland)

3.6.70 **Italy** (1) 1 **Sweden** (0) 0 *Toluca*

Italy: Albertosi; Burgnich, Facchetti, Cera, Niccolai (Rosato), Bertini, Riva, Domenghini (1), Mazzola, Di Sisti, Boninsegna
Sweden: Hellstrom; Axelsson, Nordqvist, Grip, Svensson, Bo Larsson (Nicklasson), Eriksson (Ejderstedt), Kindvall, Grahn, Cronqvist, Olsson
Referee: Taylor (England)

6.6.70 **Uruguay** (0) 0 **Italy** (0) 0 *Puebla*

Uruguay: Mazurkiewicz; Ancheta, Matosas, Ubinas, Montero Castillo, Mujica, Cubilla, Esparrago, Maneiro, Bareno (Zubia), Cortes
Italy: Albertosi; Burgnich, Facchetti, Cera, Rosato, Bertini, Riva, Domenghini (Furino), Mazzola, De Sisti, Boninsenga
Referee: Glockner (East Germany)

7.6.70 **Sweden** (0) 1 **Israel** (0) 1 *Toluca*

Sweden: Larsson S. G.; Selander, Axelsson, Olsson, Grip, Svensson, Bo Larsson, Nordahl, Kindvall, Persson (Palsson), Turesson (1)
Israel: Vissoker; Bar, Schwager, Rosen, Rosenthal, Primo, Spiegel, Vollach (Schuruk), Spiegler (1), Faygenbaum, Shum *Referee:* Tarekegn (Ethiopia)

10.6.70 **Sweden** (0) 1 **Uruguay** (0) 0 *Puebla*

Sweden: Larsson S. G.; Selander, Axelsson, Nordqvist, Grip, Svensson, Bo Larsson, Kriksson, Kindvall (Turesson), Persson, Nicklasson (Grahn (1))
Uruguay: Mazurkiewicz; Ancheta, Matosas, Ubinas, Montero Castillo, Mujica, Esparrago (Fontes), Maneiro, Zubia, Cortes, Losado
Referee: Landauer (USA)

11.6.70 **Italy** (0) 0 **Israel** (0) 0 *Toluca*

Italy: Albertosi; Burgnich, Facchetti, Cera, Rosato, Bertini, Riva, Domenghini (Rivera), Mazzola, De Sisti, Boninsegna
Israel: Vissoker; Bar, Bello, Primo, Rosen, Rosenthal, Shum, Spiegel, Faygenbaum (Rom), Spiegler, Schwager *Referee:* De Moraes (Brazil)

	P	W	D	L	F	A	Pts
Italy	3	1	2	0	1	0	4
Uruguay	3	1	1	1	2	1	3
Sweden	3	1	1	1	2	2	3
Israel	3	0	2	1	1	3	2

GROUP 3

2.6.70 **England** (0) 1 **Rumania** (0) 0 *Guadalajara*

England: Banks; Newton (Wright), Cooper, Mullery, Labone, Moore, Lee (Osgood), Ball, Hurst (1), Charlton R., Peters
Rumania: Adamache; Satmareanu, Lupescu, Dinu, Mocanu, Dumitru, Tataru (Neagu), Nunweiler, Dembrovschi, Dumitrache, Lucescu
Referee: Loraux (Belgium)

3.6.70 **Brazil** (1) **4 Czechoslovakia** (1) 1 *Guadalajara*

Brazil: Felix; Carlos Alberto, Brito, Piazza, Everaldo, Clodoaldo, Gerson (Paulo Cesar), Rivelino (1), Jairzinho (2), Tostao, Pele (1)
Czechoslovakia: Viktor; Dobias, Migas, Horvath, Hagara, Kuna, Hrdlicka (Kvasnak), Vesely F. (Vesely B.), Petras (1), Adamec, Jokl
Referee: Barreto (Uruguay)

6.6.70 **Rumania** (0) 2 **Czechoslovakia** (1) 1 *Guadalajara*

Rumania: Adamache; Satmareanu, Dinu, Lupescu, Mocanu, Dumitru (Gherghely), Nunweiler, Dembrovschi, Neagu (1), Dumitrache (pen.), Lucescu (Tataru)
Czechoslovakia: Vencel; Dobias, Migas, Horvath, Zlocha, Kuna, Kvasnak, Vesely B., Jurkanin (Adamec), Petras (1), Jokl (Vesely F.)
Referee: De Leo (Mexico)

7.6.70 **Brazil** (0) 1 **England** (0) 0 *Guadalajara*

Brazil: Felix; Carlos Alberto, Brito, Piazza, Everaldo, Clodoaldo, Paulo Cesar, Rivelino, Jairzinho (1), Tostao (Roberto), Pele
England: Banks; Wright, Cooper, Mullery, Labone, Moore, Lee (Astle), Ball, Charlton R. (Bell), Hurst, Peters *Referee:* Klein (Israel)

Jairzinho, Brazil, is the only player (other than Just Fontaine for France in 1958) to have scored in all matches. He achieved 7 goals in 1970.

10.6.70 **Brazil** (2) 3 **Rumania** (1) 2 *Guadalajara*

Brazil: Felix; Carlos Alberto, Brito, Fontana, Everaldo (Marco Antonio), Clodoaldo (Edu), Piazza, Paulo Cesar, Jairzinho (1), Tostao, Pele (2)
Rumania: Adamache (Raducanu); Satmareanu, Lupescu, Dinu, Mocanu, Dumitru, Nunweiler, Dembrovschi (1), Lucescu, Neagu, Dumitrache (1) (Tataru) *Referee:* Marschall (Austria)

11.6.70 **England** (0) 1 **Czechoslovakia** (0) 0 *Guadalajara*

England: Banks; Newton, Cooper, Mullery, Charlton J., Moore, Bell, Clarke (pen.), Astle (Osgood), Charlton R. (Ball), Peters
Czechoslovakia: Viktor; Dobias, Hrivnak, Migas, Hagara, Pollak, Kuna, Vesely F., Petras, Adamec, Capkovic (Jokl) *Referee:* Machin (France)

	P	W	D	L	F	A	Pts
Brazil	3	3	0	0	8	3	6
England	3	2	0	1	2	1	4
Rumania	3	1	0	2	4	5	2
Czechoslovakia	3	0	0	3	2	7	0

GROUP 4

2.6.70 **Peru** (0) 3 **Bulgaria** (1) 2 *Leon*

Peru: Rubinos; Campos (Gonzalez J.), De la Torre, Chumpitaz (1), Fuentes, Mifflin, Challe, Baylon (Sotil), Leon, Cubillas (1), Gallardo (1)
Bulgaria: Simeonov; Chalamanov, Dimitrov, Davidov, Aladjov, Penev, Bonev (1) (Asparoukhov), Yakimov, Popov (Marachliev), Jekov, Dermendjiev (1) *Referee:* Sbardella (Italy)

3.6.70 **West Germany** (0) 2 **Morocco** (1) 1 *Leon*

West Germany: Maier; Vogts, Schulz, Fichtel, Hottges (Lohr), Haller (Grabowski), Beckenbauer, Overath, Seeler (1), Muller (1), Held
Morocco: Allal; Abdallah, Boujemaa, Khannoussi, Slimani, Maaroufi, Bamous (Faras), El Filali, Said, Ghazouani (Abdelkader), Houmane (1)
Referee: Van Ravens (Netherlands)

6.6.70 **Peru** (0) 3 **Morocco** (0) 0 *Leon*

Peru: Rubinos; Gonzales P., De la Torre, Chumpitaz, Fuentes, Mifflin (Cruzado), Challe (1), Sotil, Leon, Cubillas (2), Gallardo (Ramirez)
Morocco: as 3.6.70 – Boujemaa (Fadili), Said (Alaoui)
Referee: Bahkramov (USSR)

7.6.70 **West Germany** (2) 5 **Bulgaria** (1) 2 *Leon*

West Germany: Maier; Vogts, Fichtel, Schnellinger, Hottges, Seeler (1), Beckenbauer (Weber), Overath, Libuda (1), Muller (3, 1 pen.), Lohr (Grabowski)
Bulgaria: Simeonov; Gaidarski, Jetchev, Nikodimov (1), Gaganelov (Chalamonov), Penev, Bonev, Kolev (1), Marachliev, Asparoukhov, Dermendjiev (Mitkov) *Referee:* De Mendibil (Spain)

10.6.70 **West Germany** (3) 3 **Peru** (1) 1 *Leon*

West Germany: as 7.6.70 – Hottges (Patzke), Libuda (Grabowski) – Muller (3)
Peru: as 6.6.70 – Challe (Cruzado), Leon (Ramirez) – Cubillas (1)
Referee: Aguilar (Mexico)

11.6.70 **Bulgaria** (1) 1 **Morocco** (0) 1 *Leon*

Bulgaria: Yordanov; Chalamanov, Penev (Dimitrov), Jetchev (1), Gaidarski, Kolev, Nikodimov, Yakimov (Bonev), Popov, Asparoukhov, Mitkov
Morocco: Hazzaz; Fadili, Slimani, Khannoussi, Boujemaa, Maaroufi, Bamous (Choukri), El Filali, Said, Alaoui (Faras), Ghazouani (1)
Referee: Saldanha (Portugal)

	P	W	D	L	F	A	Pts
West Germany	3	3	0	0	10	4	6
Peru	3	2	0	1	7	5	4
Bulgaria	3	0	1	2	5	9	1
Morocco	3	0	1	2	2	6	1

QUARTER-FINALS

14.6.70 **Uruguay** (0) 1 **USSR** (0) 0 (0-0 at 90 mins) *Mexico City*

Uruguay: Mazurkiewicz; Ancheta, Matosas, Ubinas, Montero Castillo, Mujica, Cubilla, Maneiro, Morales (Gomez), Fontes (Esparrago (1)), Cortes
USSR: as 6.6.70 – Khurtsilava (Logofet), Asatiani (Kiselev)
Referee: Van Ravens (Netherlands)

14.6.70 **Italy** (1) **4 Mexico** (1) 1 *Toluca*

Italy: as 11.6.70 – Domenghini (1) (Gori), Mazzola (Rivera (1)) – Riva (2)
Mexico: as 11.6.70 – Munguia (Diaz), Gonzalez (1) (Borja)
Referee: Scheurer (Switzerland)

Mario Zagalo is the only man to have won World Cup honours as a player and then achieved similar fame as a manager. He played in Brazil's 1958 and 1962 World Cup winning teams and then coached their successful 1970 side.

14.6.70 **Brazil** (2) **4 Peru** (1) 2 *Guadalajara*

Brazil: Felix; Carlos Alberto, Brito, Piazza, Marco Antonio, Clodoaldo, Gerson (Paulo Cesar), Rivelino (1), Jairzinho (1) (Roberto), Tostao (2), Pele
Peru: Rubinos; Campos, Fernandez, Chumpitaz, Fuentes, Challe, Mifflin, Baylon (Sotil), Leon (Reyes), Cubillas (1), Gallardo (1)
Referee: Loraux (Belgium)

14.6.70 **West Germany** (0) 3 **England** (2) 2 (2-2 at 90 mins) *Leon*
West Germany: as 10.6.70 – Hottges (Schulz), Libuda (Grabowski) – Beckenbauer (1), Seeler (1), Muller (1)

England: Bonetti; Newton, Cooper, Mullery (1), Labone, Moore, Lee, Ball, Hurst, Charlton R. (Bell), Peters (1) (Hunter) *Referee:* Coerezza (Argentina)

SEMI-FINALS

17.6.70 **Italy** (1) **4 West Germany** (0) 3 (1-1 at 90 mins) *Mexico City*

Italy: as quarter-final – Rosatto (Poletti), Mazzola (Rivera (1)) – Burgnich (1), Boninsegna (1), Riva (1)
West Germany: Maier; Vogts, Schnellinger (1), Schulz, Patzke (Held), Beckenbauer, Overath, Grabowski, Seeler, Muller (2), Lohr (Libuda)
Referee: Yamasaki (Peru)

17.6.70 **Brazil** (1) 3 **Uruguay** (1) 1 *Guadalajara*

Brazil: Felix; Carlos Alberto, Brito, Piazza, Everaldo, Clodoaldo (1), Gerson, Rivelino (1), Jairzinho (1), Tostao, Pele
Uruguay: Mazurkiewicz; Ubinas, Ancheta, Matosas, Mujica, Montero Castillo, Maneiro (Esparrago), Cortes, Cubilla (1), Fontes, Morales
Referee: De Mendibil (Spain)

MATCH FOR THIRD PLACE

20.6.70 **West Germany** (1) 1 **Uruguay** (0) 0 *Mexico City*

West Germany: Wolter; Patzke, Weber, Schnellinger (Lorenz), Fichtel, Vogts, Overath (1), Libuda (Lohr), Seeler, Muller, Held
Uruguay: as semi-final – Maneiro (Sandoval), Fontes (Esparrago)
Referee: Sbardella (Italy)

FINAL

21.6.70 **Brazil** (1) **4 Italy** (1) 1 *Mexico City* Attendance: 107,412

Brazil: as semi-final, Alberto (1), Gerson (1), Jairzinho (1), Pele (1)
Italy: as semi-final – Bertini (Juliano), Boninsegna (1) (Rivera)
Referee: Glockner (East Germany)

The only country to be present in all 12 tournaments is Brazil. Their 3 titles in 1958, 1962 and 1970 are also a record.

1974

FIFA's technical study of the tournament in West Germany revealed that the 2 teams which consistently produced the highest ratio of penetrating attacks were the finalists West Germany and the Netherlands.' But attacks are one thing, scoring goals another. Of the 3 goals in the final, 2 were penalties, and the Dutch concept of 'total football' (players off the ball running at full stretch in support of each other) was let down by poor finishing.

Even in their single goal defeat by East Germany, the West Germans had 23 attempts at scoring, 15 of them from inside the penalty area. Holland's highlight (in what proved to be a goal-less draw) was when they mounted 61 penetrating attacks against Sweden and had 36 shots, again 15 inside the area.

Scotland, the only British qualifier, remained unbeaten but were eliminated after failing to score sufficient goals against Zaire. Yugoslavia did better with 9 goals in a game against the Africans who had a man sent off (one of five dismissed in the finals, though there were 84 players cautioned).

West Germany's ultimate success owed much to the skill of Manager Helmut Schoen, the defensive organisation of Franz Beckenbauer, the winning goal from Gerd Muller whose quick check, turn and shot typified his lethal finish in the penalty area, and the sense of the team never to play outside its limitations.

1974 FIRST FINAL ROUND

GROUP 1

14.6.74 **West Germany** (1) 1 **Chile** (0) 0 *Berlin*

West Germany: Maier; Vogts, Schwarzenbeck, Beckenbauer, Breitner (1), Hoeness, Cullmann, Overath (Holzenbein), Grabowski, Muller, Heynckes
Chile: Vallejos; Garcia, Figueroa, Quintano, Arias, Valdes (Veliz), Rodriguez (Lara), Reinoso, Caszely, Ahumada, Paez
Referee: Babacan (Turkey)

14.6.74 **East Germany** (0) 2 **Australia** (0) 0 *Hamburg*

East Germany: Croy; Kische, Bransch, Weise, Watzlich, Sparwasser, Irmscher, Pommerenke, Lowe (Hoffmann), Streich (1), Vogel
Australia: Reilly; Utjesenovic, Schafer, Wilson, Curran (o.g.), Richards, Mackay, Rooney, Warren, Alston, Buljevic *Referee:* N'Diaye (Senegal)

Helmut Schoen, West Germany, is the most successful World Cup coach, having taken his team to runners-up in 1966, third in 1970 and winners in 1974.

18.6.74 **West Germany** (2) 3 **Australia** (0) 0 *Hamburg*

West Germany: as 14.6.74 – Cullmann (1) (Wimmer), Heynckes (Holzenbein) – Overath (1), Muller (1)
Australia: Reilly; Utjesenovic, Schafer, Wilson, Curran, Richards, Rooney, Mackay, Campbell (Abonyi), Alston, Buljevic (Ollerton)
Referee: Kamel (Egypt)

18.6.74 **Chile** (0) 1 **East Germany** (0) 1 *Berlin*

Chile: Vallejos; Garcia, Figueroa, Quintano, Arias, Valdes (Yavar), Reinoso, Paez, Socias (Farias), Ahumada (1), Veliz
East Germany: Croy; Kische, Bransch, Weise, Watzlich, Seguin (Kreische), Irmscher, Sparwasser, Hoffmann (1), Streich, Vogel (Ducke)
Referee: Angonese (Italy)

22.6.74 **Australia** (0) 0 **Chile** (0) 0 *Berlin*

Australia: Reilly; Utjesenovic, Wilson, Schafer, Curran (Williams), Richards, Rooney, Mackay, Abonyi, Alston (Ollerton), Buljevic
Chile: Vallejos; Garcia, Quintano, Figueroa, Arias, Paez, Caszely, Reinoso, Valdes (Farias), Ahumada, Veliz (Yavar)
Referee: Namdar (Iran)

22.6.74 **East Germany** (0) 1 **West Germany** (0) 0 *Hamburg*

East Germany: Croy; Kische, Weise, Bransch, Watzlich, Lauck, Irmscher (Hamann), Kreische, Kurbjuweit, Sparwasser (1), Hoffmann
West Germany: Maier; Vogts, Schwarzenbeck (Hottges), Beckenbauer, Breitner, Hoeness, Cullmann, Overath (Netzer), Grabowski, Muller, Flohe
Referee: Barreto (Uruguay)

	P	W	D	L	F	A	Pts
East Germany	3	2	1	0	4	1	5
West Germany	3	2	0	1	4	1	4
Chile	3	0	2	1	1	2	2
Australia	3	0	1	2	0	5	1

GROUP 2

13.6.74 **Yugoslavia** (0) 0 **Brazil** (0) 0 *Frankfurt*

Yugoslavia: Maric; Buljan, Katalinski, Bogicevic, Hadziabdic, Muzinic, Oblak, Acimovic, Petkovic, Surjak, Dzajic
Brazil: Leao; Nelinho, Mario Marinho, Pereira, Francesco Marinho, Piazza, Rivelino, Paulo Cesar L., Valdomiro, Jairzinho, Leivinha
Referee: Scheurer (Switzerland)

14.6.74 **Scotland** (2) 2 **Zaire** (0) 0 *Dortmund*

Scotland: Harvey; Jardine, McGrain, Bremner, Holton, Blackley, Dalglish (Hutchison), Hay, Lorimer (1), Jordan (1), Law
Zaire: Kazadi; Mwepu, Mukombo, Buhanga, Lobilo, Kilasu, Myanga (Kembo), Mana, Ndaye, Kidumu (Kibonge), Kakoko
Referee: Schulenberg (West Germany)

Only 2 managers have taken different teams to World Cup final tournaments. Rudolf Vytlacil a Czechoslovakian was in charge of his own country when they finished runners-up to Brazil in 1962 and 4 years later led Bulgaria in the competition. Blagoje Vidinic was the coach to Morocco in 1970 and Zaire in 1974. He was a Yugoslavian.

18.6.74 **Yugoslavia** (6) 9 **Zaire** (0) 0 *Gelsenkirchen*

Yugoslavia: Maric; Buljan, Katalinski (1), Bogicevic (1), Hadziabdic, Acimovic, Oblak (1), Surjak (1), Petkovic (1), Bajevic (3), Dzajic (1)
Zaire: Kazadi (Tubilandu); Mwepo, Mukombo, Buhanga, Lobilo, Kilasu, Ndaye, Mana, Kembo, Kidumu, Kakoko (Myanga)
Referee: Delgado (Colombia)

18.6.74 **Scotland** (0) 0 **Brazil** (0) 0 *Frankfurt*

Scotland: Harvey; Jardine, McGrain, Buchan, Holton, Bremner, Dalglish, Hay, Jordan, Lorimer, Morgan
Brazil: Leao; Nelinho, Pereira, Mario Marinho, Francesco Marinho, Piazza, Rivelino, Paulo Cesar L., Jairzinho, Mirandinha, Leivinha (Paulo Cesar C.)
Referee: Van Gemert (Netherlands)

22.6.74 **Brazil** (1) 3 **Zaire** (0) 0 *Gelsenkirchen*

Brazil: Leao; Nelinho, Pereira, Mario Marinho, Francesco Marinho, Piazza (Mirandinha), Rivelino (1), Paulo Cesar C., Jairzinho (1), Leivinha (Valdomiro (1)), Edu
Zaire: Kazadi; Mwepu, Mukombo, Buhanga, Lobilo, Kobonge, Tshinabu (Kembo), Mana, Ntumba, Kidumu (Kilasu), Myanga
Referee: Rainea (Rumania)

22.6.74 **Yugoslavia** (0) 1 **Scotland** (0) 1 *Frankfurt*

Yugoslavia: as 18.6.74 – Bajevic (Karasi (1))
Scotland: as 18.6.74 – Dalglish (Hutchison) – Jordan (1)
Referee: Archundia (Mexico)

	P	W	D	L	F	A	Pts
Yugoslavia	3	1	2	0	10	1	4
Brazil	3	1	2	0	3	0	4
Scotland	3	1	2	0	3	1	4
Zaire	3	0	0	3	0	14	0

GROUP 3

15.6.74 **Netherlands** (1) 2 **Uruguay** (0) 0 *Hannover*

Netherlands: Jongbloed; Suurbier, Rijsbergen, Haan, Krol, Jansen, Neeskens, Van Hanegem, Rep (2), Cruyff, Rensenbrink
Uruguay: Mazurkiewicz; Forlan, Masnik, Juaregui, Pavoni, Esparrago, Montero Castillo, Rocha, Cubilla (Milar), Morena, Mantegazza
Referee: Palotai (Hungary)

15.6.74 **Sweden** (0) 0 **Bulgaria** (0) 0 *Dusseldorf*

Sweden: Hellstrom; Olsson, Karlsson, Bo Larsson, Andersson, Grahn, Kindvall (Magnusson), Tapper, Torstensson, Sandberg, Edstrom
Bulgaria: Goranov; Vassilev Z., Ivkov, Penev, Velitschkov, Kolev, Bonev, Nikodimov, Voinov (Michailov), Panov (Vassilev M.), Denev
Referee: Nunez (Peru)

19.6.74 **Netherlands** (0) 0 **Sweden** (0) 0 *Dortmund*

Netherlands: Jongbloed; Suurbier, Rijsbergen, Haan, Krol, Jansen, Neeskens, Van Hanegem (De Jong), Rep, Cruyff, Keizer
Sweden: Hellstrom; Olsson (Grip), Andersson, Karlsson, Nordqvist, Tapper (Persson), Grahn, Bo Larsson, Ejderstedt, Edstrom, Sandberg
Referee: Winsemann (Canada)

19.6.74 **Bulgaria** (1) 1 **Uruguay** (0) 1 *Hannover*

Bulgaria: as 15.6.74 – Nikodimov (Michailov) – Bonev (1)
Uruguay: Mazurkiewicz; Forlan, Garisto (Masnik), Jauregui, Pavoni (1), Esparrago, Mantegazza (Cardaccio), Rocha, Milar, Morena, Corbo
Referee: Taylor (England)

23.6.74 **Netherlands** (2) 4 **Bulgaria** (0) 1 *Dortmund*

Netherlands: as 15.6.74 – Neeskens (2) (De Jong (o.g.)), Van Hanegem (Israel) – Krol (1), Rep (1)
Bulgaria: Staikov; Vassilev Z., Ivkov, Penev, Velitschkov, Kolev, Bonev, Stoyanov (Michailov), Voinov, Panov (Borissov), Denev
Referee: Boskovic (Australia)

23.6.74 **Sweden** (0) 3 **Uruguay** (0) 0 *Dusseldorf*

Sweden: Hellstrom; Andersson, Nordqvist, Karlsson, Grip, Grahn, Kindvall (Torstensson), Bo Larsson, Magnusson (Ahlstrom), Edstrom (2), Sandberg (1)
Uruguay: as 19.6.74 – Garisto (Masnik), Corbo (Cubilla)
Referee: Linemayr (Austria)

	P	W	D	L	F	A	Pts
Netherlands	3	2	1	0	6	1	5
Sweden	3	1	2	0	3	0	4
Bulgaria	3	0	2	1	2	5	2
Uruguay	3	0	1	2	1	6	1

GROUP 4

15.6.74 **Italy** (0) 3 **Haiti** (0) 1 *Munich*

Italy: Zoff; Spinosi, Morini, Burgnich, Facchetti, Mazzola, Capello, Rivera (1), Benetti (1), Chinaglia (Anastasi (1)), Riva
Haiti: Francillon; Bayonne, Nazaire, Jean-Joseph, Auguste, Francois, Vorbe, Desir, Antoine, Saint-Vil G. (Barthelmy), Sanon (1)
Referee: Llobregat (Venezuela)

15.6.74 **Poland** (2) 3 **Argentina** (0) 2 *Stuttgart*

Poland: Tomaszewski; Szymanowski, Zmuda, Gorgon, Musial, Kasperczyk, Maszczyk, Deyna, Lato (2), Szarmach (1) (Domarski), Gadocha (Cmikiewicz)
Argentina: Carnevali; Wolff, Perfumo, Heredia (1), Sa, Bargas (Telch), Brindisi (Houseman), Babington (1), Balbuena, Ayala, Kempes
Referee: Thomas (Wales)

The two players with the shortest names to have appeared in a World Cup final tournament are Cavetano Re (Paraguay) in 1958 and Francisco Sa (Argentina) in 1974.

19.6.74 **Poland** (5) 7 **Haiti** (0) 0 *Munich*

Poland: as 15.6.74 – Musial (Gut), Maszczyk (Cmikiewicz) – Gorgon (1), Deyna (1), Lato (2), Szarmach (3)
Haiti: Francillon; Bayonne, Nazaire, Vorbe, Auguste, Francois, Desir, Andre (Barthelemy), Sanon, Antoine, Saint-Vil R. (Racine)
Referee: Suppiah (Singapore)

19.6.74 **Argentina** (1) 1 **Italy** (1) 1 *Stuttgart*

Argentina: Carnevali; Wolff (Glaria), Perfumo (o.g.), Heredia, Sa, Telch, Houseman (1), Babington, Ayala, Kempes, Yazalde (Chazarreta)
Italy: Zoff; Spinosi, Morini (Wilson), Burgnich, Facchetti, Mazzola, Capello, Rivera (Causio), Benetti, Riva, Anastasi *Referee:* Kasakov (USSR)

23.6.74 **Argentina** (2) 4 **Haiti** (0) 1 *Munich*

Argentina: as 19.6.74 – Houseman (1) (Brindisi), Kempes (Balbuena) – Yazalde (2), Ayala (1)
Haiti: Francillon; Ducoste, Bayonne, Nazaire (Leandre M.), Louis, Vorbe, Desir, Saint-Vil G. (Leandre F.), Antoine, Racine, Sanon (1)
Referee: Sanchez-Ibanez (Spain)

23.6.74 **Poland** (2) 2 **Italy** (0) 1 *Stuttgart*

Poland: as other Group 4 matches – Szarmach (1) (Cmikiewicz) – Deyna (1)
Italy: Zoff; Spinosi, Morini, Burgnich (Wilson), Facchetti, Mazzola, Benetti, Capello (1), Causio, Chinaglia (Boninsegna), Anastasi
Referee: Weyland (West Germany)

	P	W	D	L	F	A	Pts
Poland	3	3	0	0	12	3	6
Argentina	3	1	1	1	7	5	3
Italy	3	1	1	1	5	4	3
Haiti	3	0	0	3	2	14	0

SECOND FINAL ROUND

GROUP A

26.6.74 **Brazil** (0) 1 **East Germany** (0) 0 *Hannover*

Brazil: Leao; Pereira, Ze Maria, Mario Marinho, Francesco Marinho, Rivelino (1), Paulo Cesar C., Paulo Cesar L., Valdomiro, Jairzinho, Dirceu
East Germany: Croy; Kische, Bransch, Weise, Watzlich, Lauck (Lowe), Hamann (Irmscher), Kurbjuweit, Streich, Sparwasser, Hoffmann
Referee: Thomas (Wales)

26.6.74 **Netherlands** (2) 4 **Argentina** (0) 0 *Gelsenkirchen*

Netherlands: Jongbloed; Suurbier (Israel), Rijsbergen, Haan, Krol (1), Jansen, Neeskens, Van Hanegem, Rep (1), Cruyff (2), Rensenbrink
Argentina: Carnevali; Wolff (Glaria), Perfumo, Heredia, Sa, Telch, Balbuena, Squeo, Yazalde, Ayala, Houseman (Kempes) *Referee:* Davidson (Scotland)

30.6.74 **Netherlands** (1) 2 **East Germany** (0) 0 *Gelsenkirchen*

Netherlands: as 26.6.74 – no substitutes – Neeskens (1), Rensenbrink (1)
East Germany: Croy; Kische, Weise, Bransch, Kurbjuweit, Lauck (Kreische), Schnuphase, Sparwasser, Pommerenke, Lowe (Ducke), Hoffmann
Referee: Scheurer (Switzerland)

30.6.74 **Brazil** (1) 2 **Argentina** (1) 1 *Hannover*

Brazil: as 26.6.74, Rivelino (1), Jairzinho (1)
Argentina: Carnevali; Glaria, Bargas, Heredia, Sa (Carrascosa), Brindisi (1), Squeo, Babington, Balbuena, Ayala, Kempes (Houseman)
Referee: Loraux (Belgium)

3.7.74 **Netherlands** (0) 2 **Brazil** (0) 0 *Dortmund*

Netherlands: as other Group A matches – Neeskens (1) (Israel), Rensenbrink (De Jong) – Cruyff (1)
Brazil: as other Group A matches – Paulo Cesar L. (Mirandinha)
Referee: Tschenscher (West Germany)

3.7.74 **East Germany** (1) 1 **Argentina** (1) 1 *Gelsenkirchen*

East Germany: Croy; Kische, Weise, Bransch, Kurbjuweit, Sparwasser, Schnuphase, Pommerenke, Lowe (Vogel), Streich (1) (Ducke), Hoffmann
Argentina: Fillol; Wolff, Heredia, Bargas, Carrascosa, Telch, Brindisi, Babington, Houseman (1), Ayala, Kempes *Referee:* Taylor (England)

	P	W	D	L	F	A	Pts
Netherlands	3	3	0	0	8	0	6
Brazil	3	2	0	1	3	3	4
East Germany	3	0	1	2	1	4	1
Argentina	3	0	1	2	2	7	1

GROUP B

26.6.74 **West Germany** (1) 2 **Yugoslavia** (0) 0 *Dusseldorf*

West Germany: Maier; Vogts, Schwarzenbeck, Beckenbauer, Breitner (1), Wimmer (Hoeness), Overath, Bonhof, Holzenbein (Flohe), Muller (1), Herzog
Yugoslavia: Maric; Buljan, Katalinski, Muzinic, Hadziabdic, Oblak (Jerkovic), Acimovic, Surjak, Popivoda, Karasi, Dzajic (Petkovic)
Referee: Marques (Brazil)

26.6.74 **Poland** (1) 1 **Sweden** (0) 0 *Stuttgart*

Poland: Tomaszewski; Gut, Gorgon, Szymanowski, Zmuda, Kasperczak, Deyna, Maszczyk, Lato (1), Szarmach (Kmiecik), Gadocha
Sweden: Hellstrom; Andersson (Augustsson), Grip, Karlsson, Nordqvist, Bo Larsson, Torstensson, Tapper (Ahlstrom), Edstrom, Grahn, Sandberg
Referee: Barreto (Uruguay)

30.6.74 **West Germany** (0) 4 **Sweden** (1) 2 *Dusseldorf*

West Germany: Maier; Vogts, Schwarzenbeck, Beckenbauer, Breitner, Hoeness (pen.), Bonhof (1), Overath (1), Holzenbein (Flohe), Muller, Herzog (Grabowski (1))
Sweden: Hellstrom; Olsson, Karlsson, Nordqvist, Augustsson, Tapper, Bo Larsson (Ejderstedt), Grahn, Torstensson, Edstrom (1), Sandberg (1)
Referee: Kasakov (USSR)

30.6.74 **Poland** (1) 2 **Yugoslavia** (1) 1 *Frankfurt*

Poland: return to winning Group 4 team – Deyna (pen.) (Domarski), Szarmach (Cmikiewicz) – Lato (1)
Yugoslavia: Maric; Buljan, Katalinski, Bogicevic, Hadziabdic, Karasi (1), Oblak (Jerkovic), Acimovic, Petkovic (Petkovic), Bajevic, Surjak
Referee: Glockner (East Germany)

3.7.74 **Sweden** (1) 2 **Yugoslavia** (1) 1 *Dusseldorf*

Sweden: Hellstrom; Olsson, Karlsson, Nordqvist, Augustsson, Tapper, Grahn, Persson, Torstensson (1), Edstrom (1), Sandberg
Yugoslavia: Maric; Buljan, Katalinski, Hadziabdic, Pavlovic (Peruzovic), Bogicevic, Acimovic, Jerkovic, Petrovic (Karasi), Surjak (1), Dzajic
Referee: Pestarino (Argentina)

Gerd Muller, West Germany, holds the aggregate goalscoring record in final tournaments. His total of 14 goals came from 10 in 1970 and 4 in 1974. In qualifying and final series games in the 1970 competition he scored 19 goals.

3.7.74 **West Germany** (0) 1 **Poland** (0) 0 *Frankfurt*

West Germany: Maier; Vogts, Schwarzenbeck, Beckenbauer, Breitner, Hoeness, Bonhof, Overath, Grabowski, Muller (1), Holzenbein
Poland: Tomaszewski; Szymanowski, Gorgon, Zmuda, Musial, Kasperczyk (Cmikiewicz), Deyna, Maszczyk (Kmiecik), Lato, Domarski, Gadocha
Referee: Linemayr (Austria)

	P	W	D	L	F	A	Pts
West Germany	3	3	0	0	7	2	6
Poland	3	2	0	1	3	2	4
Sweden	3	1	0	2	4	6	2
Yugoslavia	3	0	0	3	2	6	0

MATCH FOR THIRD PLACE

6.7.74 **Poland** (0) 1 **Brazil** (0) 0 *Munich*

Poland: return to winning Group 4 team – Kasperczak (Cmikiewicz), Szarmach (Kapka) – Lato (1)
Brazil: Leao; Ze Maria, Alfredo, Mario Marinho, Francesco Marinho, Rivelino, Paulo Cesar C., Ademir (Mirandinha), Valdomiro, Jairzinho, Dirceu *Referee:* Angonese (Italy)

FINAL

7.7.74 **West Germany** (2) 2 **Netherlands** (1) 1 *Munich* Attendance: 77,833

West Germany: as 3.7.74, Breitner (pen.), Muller (1)
Netherlands: as winning Group A team – Rijsbergen (De Jong), Rensenbrink (Van de Kerkhof R.) – Neeskens (pen.)
Referee: Taylor (England)

1978

Argentina became the third host nation to win the competition in 4 Cups, in a tense but flowing final in which the Dutch, though forcing extra time, again had to be content with runners-up medals.

Although 102 goals were scored the average was only slightly better than the all-time low of 1974, with the gap widening between improved but uncompromising defences and impoverished attacks.

Only 2 goals came from free-kicks and just one following a corner, though several memorable long-range efforts succeeded from open play. There were 3 own goals, 3 players sent off and 58 cautioned.

Of 14 penalty kicks awarded, only 2 failed, including Kazimierz Deyna's for Poland against Argentina in his 100th international (the referee's decision to re-position the ball quite possibly disturbed his concentration). Scotland, the other spot-kick failures, showed their inconsistency in losing to Peru, being held by Iran and then beating the Netherlands when survival hopes were vanishing.

Brazil, the only unbeaten side, finished third and conceded just 3 goals. A disallowed effort from a corner kick in the last minute of their match against Sweden cued both on and off-the-field upsets.

After the Brazilians had beaten Poland 3-1 the Argentines knew that they needed a margin of 4 goals to beat Peru four hours later, and reach the final. They hit 6.

1978 FIRST FINAL ROUND

GROUP 1

2.6.78 **Argentina** (1) 2 **Hungary** (1) 1 *Buenos Aires*

Argentina: Fillol; Olguin, Luis Galvan, Passarella, Tarantini, Ardiles, Gallego, Valencia (Alonso), Houseman (Bertoni (1)), Luque (1), Kempes
Hungary: Gujdar; Torok (Martos), Kereki, Kocsis, Toth J., Nyilasi, Pinter, Zombori, Csapo (1), Torocsik, Nagy *Referee:* Garrido (Portugal)

2.6.78 **Italy** (1) 2 **France** (1) 1 *Mar del Plata*

Italy: Zoff; Scirea, Gentile, Bellugi, Cabrini, Benetti, Causio, Tardelli, Antognoni (Zaccarelli (1)), Rossi (1), Bettega
France: Bertrand-Demanes; Tresor, Janvion, Rio, Bossis, Guillou, Michel, Platino, Dalger, Lacombe (1) (Berdoll), Six (Rouyer)
Referee: Rainea (Rumania)

6.6.78 **Argentina** (1) 2 **France** (0) 1 *Buenos Aires*

Argentina: as 2.6.78 – Valencia (Alonso then Ortiz) – Passarella (pen.), Luque (1)
France: Bertrand-Demanes (Baratelli); Tresor, Battiston, Lopez, Bossis, Bathenay, Michel, Platini (1), Rocheteau, Lacombe, Six
Referee: Dubach (Switzerland)

6.6.78 **Italy** (2) 3 **Hungary** (0) 1 *Mar del Plata*

Italy: as 2.6.78 – Cabrini (Cuccuredu), Bettega (1) (Graziani) – Benetti (1), Rossi (1)
Hungary: Meszaros; Kereki, Martos, Kocsis, Toth J., Csapo, Pinter, Zombori, Pusztai, Fazekas (Halasz), Nagy (Toth A. (pen.))
Referee: Barretto (Uruguay)

10.6.78 **Italy** (0) 1 **Argentina** (0) 0 *Buenos Aires*

Italy: as before – Bellugi (Cuccureddu), Antognoni (Zaccarelli) – Bettega (1)
Argentina: Fillol; Olguin, Luis Galvan, Passarella, Tarantini, Gallego, Ardiles, Valencia, Bertoni, Kempes, Ortiz (Houseman)
Referee: Klein (Israel)

10.6.78 **France** (3) 3 **Hungary** (1) 1 *Mar del Plata*

France: Dropsy; Tresor, Janvion, Lopez (1), Bracci, Petit, Bathenay, Papi (Platini), Rocheteau (1) (Six), Berdoll (1), Rouyer
Hungary: Gujdar; Kereki, Balint, Martos, Toth J., Nyilasi, Pinter, Zombori (1), Pusztai, Torocsik, Nagy (Csapo) *Referee:* Coehlo (Brazil)

	P	W	D	L	F	A	Pts
Italy	3	3	0	0	6	2	6
Argentina	3	2	0	1	4	3	4
France	3	1	0	2	5	5	2
Hungary	3	0	0	3	3	8	0

GROUP 2

1.6.78 **West Germany** (0) 0 **Poland** (0) 0 *Buenos Aires*

West Germany: Maier; Kaltz, Vogts, Russmann, Zimmerman, Bonhof, Beer, Flohe, Muller H., Abramczik, Fischer
Poland: Tomaszewski; Gorgon, Maculewicz, Szymanowski, Zmuda, Masztaler (Kasperczak), Nawalka, Deyna, Lato, Lubanski (Boniek), Szarmach *Referee:* Coerezza (Argentina)

2.6.78 **Tunisia** (0) 3 **Mexico** (1) 1 *Rosario*

Tunisia: Naili; Dhouieb (1), Jendoubi, Jebali, Kaabi (1), Ghommidh (1), Temine (Labidi), Agrebi, Akid, Tarak, Ben Aziza (Karoui)
Mexico: Reyes; Martinez Diaz, Vazquez Ayala (pen.), Ramos, Tena, De la Torre, Cuellar, Mendizabal (Lugo Gomez), Isiordia, Rangel, Sanchez
Referee: Gordon (Scotland)

6.6.78 **Poland** (1) 1 **Tunisia** (0) 0 *Rosario*

Poland: Tomaszewski; Gorgon, Szymanowski, Zmuda, Maculewicz, Nawalka, Deyna, Kasperczak, Lato (1), Lubanski (Boniek), Szarmach (Iwan)
Tunisia: Naili; Dhouieb, Jendoubi, Gasmi, Kaabi, Ghommidh, Temine, Agrebi, Akid, Tarak, Jebali *Referee:* Martinez (Spain)

6.6.78 **West Germany** (4) 6 **Mexico** (0) 0 *Cordoba*

West Germany: Maier; Kaltz, Vogts, Russmann, Dietz, Bonhof, Flohe (2), Muller H. (1), Rummenigge (2), Fischer, Muller D. (1)
Mexico: Reyes (Soto); Martinez Diaz, Tena, Ramos, Vazquez Ayala, Lopez Zarza (Lugo Gomez), Cuellar, De la Torre, Sanchez, Rangel, Mendizabal
Referee: Bouzo (Syria)

10.6.78 **West Germany** (0) 0 **Tunisia** (0) 0 *Cordoba*

West Germany: Maier; Kaltz, Vogts, Russmann, Dietz, Bonhof, Flohe, Rummenigge, Muller H., Fischer, Muller D.
Tunisia: Naili; Jebali, Dhouieb, Jendoubi, Kaabi, Ghommidh, Gasmi, Tarak, Agrebi, Temine, Akid (Ben Aziza) *Referee:* Orosco (Peru)

10.6.78 **Poland** (1) 3 **Mexico** (0) 1 *Rosario*

Poland: Tomaszewski; Gorgon, Szymanowski, Zmuda, Kasperczak, Deyna (1), Masztaler, Rudy (Maculewicz), Boniek (2), Lato, Iwan (Lubanski)
Mexico: Soto; Gomez C., Cisneros, De la Torre, Vazquez Ayala, Cuellar, Flores, Cardenas (Mendizabal), Ortega, Rangel (1), Sanchez
Referee: Namdar (Iran)

	P	W	D	L	F	A	Pts
Poland	3	2	1	0	4	1	5
West Germany	3	1	2	0	6	0	4
Tunisia	3	1	1	1	3	2	3
Mexico	3	0	0	3	2	12	0

GROUP 3

3.6.78 **Austria** (1) 2 **Spain** (1) 1 *Buenos Aires*

Austria: Koncilia; Pezzey, Sara, Breitenberger, Obermayer, Prohaska, Kreuz, Hickersberger (Weber), Jara, Schachner (1) (Pirkner), Krankl (1)
Spain: Miguel Angel; Marcelino, Pirri, Migueli, San Jose, De la Cruz, Asensi, Rexach (Quini), Cardenosa (Leal), Dani (1), Ruben Cano
Referee: Palotai (Hungary)

3.6.78 **Sweden** (1) 1 **Brazil** (1) 1 *Mar del Plata*

Sweden: Hellstrom; Andersson R., Borg, Nordqvist, Erlandsson, Larsson L. (Edstrom), Tapper, Linderoth, Bo Larsson, Sjoberg (1), Wendt
Brazil: Leao; Oscar, Toninho, Amaral, Edinho, Batista, Zico, Cerezo, Gil (Nelinho), Reinaldo (1), Rivelino *Referee:* Thomas (Wales)

7.6.78 **Austria** (1) 1 **Sweden** (0) 0 *Buenos Aires*

Austria: Koncilia; Obermayer, Sara, Pezzey, Breitenberger, Prohaska, Hickersberger, Krieger (Weber), Jara, Krankl (pen.), Kreuz
Sweden: as 3.6.78 – Tapper (Torstensson), Linderoth (Edstrom)
Referee: Corver (Netherlands)

7.6.78 **Brazil** (0) 0 **Spain** (0) 0 *Mar del Plata*

Brazil: Leao; Amaral, Nelinho (Gil), Oscar, Edinho, Cerezo, Batista, Zico (Mendonca), Dirceu, Toninho, Reinaldo
Spain: Miguel Angel; Olmo, Marcelino, Migueli (Biosca), Uria (Guzman), Leal, Asensi, Cardenosa, San Jose, Juanito, Santillana
Referee: Gonella (Italy)

11.6.78 **Spain** (0) 1 **Sweden** (0) 0 *Buenos Aires*

Spain: Miguel Angel; Olmo (Pirri), Marcelino, Biosca, San Jose, Uria, Leal, Asensi (1), Cardenosa, Juanito, Santillana
Sweden: Hellstrom; Andersson R., Borg, Nordqvist, Erlandsson, Larsson L., Bo Larsson, Nordin, Nilsson, Sjoberg (Linderoth), Edstrom (Wendt)
Referee: Biwersi (West Germany)

11.6.78 **Brazil** (1) 1 **Austria** (0) 0 *Mar del Plata*

Brazil: Leao; Amaral, Toninho, Oscar, Rodrigues Neto, Batista, Cerezo (Chicao), Dirceu, Gil, Mendonca (Zico), Roberto (1)
Austria: as 7.6.78 – Hickersberger (Weber), Krieger (Happich)
Referee: Wurtz (France)

	P	**W**	**D**	**L**	**F**	**A**	**Pts**
Austria	3	2	0	1	3	2	4
Brazil	3	1	2	0	2	1	4
Spain	3	1	1	1	2	2	3
Sweden	3	0	1	2	1	3	1

GROUP 4

3.6.78 **Netherlands** (1) 3 **Iran** (0) 0 *Mendoza*

Netherlands: Jongbloed; Suurbier, Rijsbergen, Krol, Haan, Jansen, Neeskens, Van de Kerkhof W., Rep, Rensenbrink (3, 2 pens.), Van de Kerkhof R. (Nanninga)
Iran: Hejazi; Nazari, Abdullahi, Kazerani, Eskandarian, Parvin, Ghassempour, Sadeghi, Nayeb-Agha, Faraki (Rowshan), Jahani
Referee: Archundia (Mexico)

3.6.78 **Peru** (1) 3 **Scotland** (1) 1 *Cordoba*

Peru: Quiroga; Chumpitaz, Duarte, Manzo, Diaz, Velasquez, Cueto (1) (Rojas), Cubillas (2), Munante, La Rosa (Sotil), Oblitas
Scotland: Rough; Kennedy, Burns, Rioch (Gemmill), Forsyth, Buchan, Dalglish, Hartford, Jordan (1), Masson (Macari), Johnston
Referee: Eriksson (Sweden)

7.6.78 **Scotland** (1) 1 **Iran** (0) 1 *Cordoba*

Scotland: Rough; Jardine, Donachie, Gemmill, Burns, Buchan (Forsyth), Dalglish (Harper), Hartford, Jordan, Macari, Robertson
Iran: Hejazi; Nazari, Abdullahi, Kazerani, Eskandarian (o.g.), Parvin, Ghassempour, Sadeghi, Danaifar (1) (Nayeb-Agha), Faraki (Rowshan), Jahani *Referee:* N'Diaye (Senegal)

7.6.78 **Netherlands** (0) 0 **Peru** (0) 0 *Mendoza*

Netherlands: Jongbloed; Suurbier, Rijsbergen, Krol, Poortvliet, Neeskens (Nanninga), Van de Kerkhof W., Jansen, Haan, Van de Kerkhof R. (Rep), Rensenbrink
Peru: as 3.6.78 – La Rosa (Sotil) *Referee:* Prokop (East Germany)

11.6.78 **Peru** (3) 4 **Iran** (1) 1 *Cordoba*

Peru: as other Group 4 matches – Manzo (Leguia), La Rosa (Sotil) – Velasquez (1), Cubillas (3, 2 pens.)
Iran: Hejazi; Nazari, Abdullahi, Kazerani, Allahvardi, Parvin, Ghassempour, Sadeghi, Danaifar, Faraki (Jahani), Rowshan (1) (Fariba)
Referee: Jarguz (Poland)

Robbie Rensenbrink, Netherlands, scored the 1,000th World Cup goal: a penalty v Scotland in 1978.

11.6.78 **Scotland** (1) 3 **Netherlands** (1) 2 *Mendoza*

Scotland: Rough; Kennedy, Donachie, Rioch, Forsyth, Buchan, Dalglish (1), Hartford, Jordan, Gemmill (2, 1 pen.), Souness
Netherlands: Jongbloed; Suurbier, Rijsbergen (Wildschut), Krol, Poortvliet, Neeskens (Boskamp), Jansen, Van de Kerkhof W., Van de Kerkhof R., Rep (1), Rensenbrink (pen.) *Referee:* Linemayr (Austria)

	P	W	D	L	F	A	Pts
Peru	3	2	1	0	7	2	5
Netherlands	3	1	1	1	5	3	3
Scotland	3	1	1	1	5	6	3
Iran	3	0	1	2	2	8	1

SECOND FINAL ROUND

GROUP A

14.6.78 **West Germany** (0) 0 **Italy** (0) 0 *Buenos Aires*

West Germany: Maier; Kaltz, Vogts, Russmann, Dietz, Bonhof, Flohe (Beer), Zimmermann (Konopka), Holzenbein, Rummenigge, Fischer
Italy: Zoff; Scirea, Gentile, Bellugi, Cabrini, Tardelli, Benetti, Antognoni (Zaccarelli), Causio, Rossi, Bettega *Referee:* Maksimovic (Yugoslavia)

14.6.78 **Netherlands** (3) 5 **Austria** (0) 1 *Cordoba*

Netherlands: Schrijvers; Wildschut, Brandts (1) (Van Kraay), Krol, Poortvliet, Jansen, Haan, Van de Kerkhof W. (1), Rep (2), Van de Kerkhof R. (Schoenaker), Rensenbrink (pen.)
Austria: Koncilia; Obermayer (1), Sara, Pezzey, Breitenberger, Hickersberger, Prohaska, Jara, Krieger, Kreuz, Krankl
Referee: Gordon (Scotland)

18.6.78 **Italy** (1) 1 **Austria** (0) 0 *Buenos Aires*

Italy: Zoff; Scirea, Bellugi (Cuccureddu), Gentile, Cabrini, Benetti, Zaccarelli, Tardelli, Causio, Rossi (1), Bettega (Graziani)
Austria: Koncilia; Obermayer, Sara, Pezzey, Strasser, Hickersberger, Prohaska, Kreuz, Krieger, Schachner (Pirkner), Krankl
Referee: Rion (Belgium)

18.6.78 **West Germany** (1) 2 **Netherlands** (1) 2 *Cordoba*

West Germany: Maier; Kaltz, Vogts, Russmann, Dietz, Bonhof, Holzenbein, Beer, Abramczik (1), Muller D. (1), Rummenigge
Netherlands: as 14.6.78 – Wildschut (Nanninga) – Haan (1), Van de Kerkhof R. (1)
Referee: Barreto (Uruguay)

21.6.78 **Netherlands** (0) 2 **Italy** (1) 1 *Buenos Aires*

Netherlands: Schrijvers (Jongbloed); Brandts (1, o.g.), Krol, Poortvliet, Jansen, Haan (1), Neeskens, Van de Kerkhof W., Van de Kerkhof R., Rep (Van Kraay), Rensenbrink
Italy: Zoff; Scirea, Gentile, Cuccureddu, Cabrini, Tardelli, Zaccarelli, Benetti (Graziani), Causio (Sala C.), Rossi, Bettega *Referee:* Martinez (Spain)

21.6.78 **Austria** (0) 3 **West Germany** (1) 2 *Cordoba*

Austria: Koncilia; Obermayer, Sara, Pezzey, Strasser, Hickersberger, Prohaska, Kreuz, Krieger, Schachner (Oberacher), Krankl (2)
West Germany: as 18.6.78 – Beer (Muller H.), Muller D. (Fischer) – Rummenigge (1), Vogts (o.g.), Holzenbein (1)
Referee: Klein (Israel)

	P	W	D	L	F	A	Pts
Netherlands	3	2	1	0	9	4	5
Italy	3	1	1	1	2	2	3
West Germany	3	0	2	1	4	5	2
Austria	3	1	0	2	4	8	2

GROUP B

14.6.78 **Argentina** (1) 2 **Poland** (0) 0 *Rosario*

Argentina: Fillol; Olguin, Luis Galvan, Passarella, Tarantini, Ardiles, Gallego, Valencia (Villa), Houseman (Ortiz), Bertoni, Kempes (2)
Poland: Tomaszewski; Kasperczak, Szymanowski, Zmuda, Maculewicz, Masztaler (Masur), Deyna, Nawalka, Boniek, Lato, Szarmach
Referee: Eriksson (Sweden)

England, with Gordon Banks in goal, conceded only 3 goals in 6 matches before winning the 1966 World Cup. But Leao of Brazil conceded only 3 in 7 matches when his country finished third in 1978 and Jan Jongbloed, Netherlands, let in 3 for the 1974 runners-up in 7 appearances.

14.6.78 **Brazil** (2) 3 **Peru** (0) 0 *Mendoza*

Brazil: as 11.6.78 – Cerezo (Chicao), Gil (Zico (pen.)) – Dirceu (2)
Peru: Quiroga; Chumpitaz, Diaz (Navarro), Manzo, Duarte, Velasquez, Cueto, Cubillas, La Rosa, Munante, Oblitas (Rojas P.)
Referee: Rainea (Rumania)

18.6.78 **Argentina** (0) 0 **Brazil** (0) 0 *Rosario*

Argentina: Fillol; Olguin, Luis Galvan, Passarella, Tarantini, Ardiles (Villa), Gallego, Ortiz (Alonso), Kempes, Bertoni, Luque
Brazil: Leao; Amaral, Toninho, Oscar, Rodrigues Neto (Edinho), Chicao, Batista, Dirceu, Mendonca (Zico), Gil, Roberto
Referee: Palotai (Hungary)

18.6.78 **Poland** (0) 1 **Peru** (0) 0 *Mendoza*

Poland: Kukla; Gorgon, Szymanowski, Zmuda, Maculewicz, Masztaler (Kasperczak), Nawalka, Deyna, Lato, Boniek (Lubanski), Szarmach (1)
Peru: Quiroga; Chumpitaz, Duarte, Manzo, Navarro, Cueto, Quezada, Cubillas, La Rosa (Sotil), Munante (Rojas P.), Oblitas
Referee: Partridge (England)

21.6.78 **Brazil** (1) 3 **Poland** (1) 1 *Mendoza*

Brazil: Leao; Amaral, Toninho, Oscar, Nelinho (1), Cerezo (Rivelino), Batista, Dirceu, Zico (Mendonca), Gil, Roberto (2)
Poland: Kukla; Gorgon, Szymanowski, Zmuda, Maculewicz, Kasperczak (Lubanski), Nawalka, Deyna, Boniek, Lato (1), Szarmach
Referee: Silvagno (Chile)

21.6.78 **Argentina** (2) 6 **Peru** (0) 0 *Rosario*

Argentina: Fillol; Olguin, Luis Galvan, Passarella, Tarantini (1), Larrosa, Gallego (Oviedo), Kempes (2), Bertoni (Houseman (1)), Luque (2), Ortiz
Peru: Quiroga; Chumpitaz, Duarte, Manzo, Rojas R., Cueto, Velasquez (Gorriti), Cubillas, Quezada, Munante, Oblitas *Referee:* Wurtz (France)

	P	**W**	**D**	**L**	**F**	**A**	**Pts**
Argentina	3	2	1	0	8	0	5
Brazil	3	2	1	0	6	1	5
Poland	3	1	0	2	2	5	2
Peru	3	0	0	3	0	10	0

MATCH FOR THIRD PLACE

24.6.78 **Brazil** (0) 2 **Italy** (1) 1 *Buenos Aires*

Brazil: Leao; Amaral, Nelinho (1), Oscar, Rodrigues Neto, Batista, Cerezo (Rivelino), Dirceu (1), Gil (Reinaldo), Roberto, Mendonca
Italy: Zoff; Scirea, Gentile, Cuccureddu, Maldera, Cabrini, Antognoni (Sala C.), Sala P., Causio (1), Rossi, Bettega *Referee:* Klein (Israel)

FINAL

25.6.78 **Argentina** (1) 3 **Netherlands** (0) 1 *Buenos Aires*
(after extra time: 1-1 at 90 mins) Attendance: 77,260

Argentina: Fillol; Olguin, Luis Galvan, Passarella, Tarantini, Ardiles (Larrosa), Gallego, Kempes (2), Bertoni (1), Luque, Ortiz (Houseman)
Netherlands: Jongbloed; Poortvliet, Krol, Brandts, Jansen (Suurbier), Neeskens, Haan, Van de Kerkhof W., Van de Kerkhof R., Rep (Nanninga (1)), Rensenbrink *Referee:* Gonella (Italy)

Table of matches in World Cup finals 1930–78

	P	W	D	L	F	A
1. Brazil	52	33	10	9	119	56
2. *West Germany	47	28	9	10	110	68
3. Italy	36	20	6	10	62	40
4. Uruguay	29	14	5	10	57	39
5. Argentina	29	14	5	10	55	43
6. Hungary	26	13	2	11	73	42
7. Sweden	28	11	6	11	48	46
8. England	24	10	6	8	34	28
9. Yugoslavia	25	10	5	10	45	34
10. USSR	19	10	3	6	30	21
11. Netherlands	16	8	3	5	32	19
12. Poland	14	9	1	4	27	17
13. Austria	18	9	1	8	33	36
14. Czechoslovakia	22	8	3	11	32	36
15. France	20	8	1	11	43	38
16. Chile	18	7	3	8	23	24
17. Spain	18	7	3	8	22	25
18. Switzerland	18	5	2	11	28	44
19. Portugal	6	5	0	1	17	8
20. Mexico	24	3	4	17	21	62
21. Peru	12	4	1	7	17	25
22. Scotland	11	2	4	5	12	21
23. East Germany	6	2	2	2	5	5
24. Paraguay	7	2	2	3	12	19
25. USA	7	3	0	4	12	21
26. Wales	5	1	3	1	4	4
27. Northern Ireland	5	2	1	2	6	10
28. Rumania	8	2	1	5	12	17
29. Bulgaria	12	0	4	8	9	29
30. Tunisia	3	1	1	1	3	2
31. North Korea	4	1	1	2	5	9
32. Cuba	3	1	1	1	5	12
33. Belgium	9	1	1	7	12	25
34. Turkey	3	1	0	2	10	11
35. Israel	3	0	2	1	1	3
36. Morocco	3	0	1	2	2	6
37. Australia	3	0	1	2	0	5
38. Iran	3	0	1	2	2	8
39. Colombia	3	0	1	2	5	11
40. Norway	1	0	0	1	1	2
41. Egypt	1	0	0	1	2	4
42. Dutch East Indies	1	0	0	1	0	6
43. El Salvador	3	0	0	3	0	9
44. South Korea	2	0	0	2	0	16
45. Haiti	3	0	0	3	2	14
46. Zaire	3	0	0	3	0	14
47. Bolivia	3	0	0	3	0	16

*including Germany 1934–1938

1982 World Cup Qualifying Rounds

There were 109 entries for the 1982 World Cup including Zimbabwe who replaced Central Africa when they were excluded for failing to pay their entrance fee. For the first time in the history of the competition there was to be an increase from 16 to 24 teams in the final stages to be held in Spain between June 13 and July 11.

Spain as the host nation and Argentina as the holders were exempted from the qualifying games which began on March 26, 1980 and ended on January 10, 1982.

The qualifying draw took place in Zurich, Switzerland on October 14, 1979 and the 108 final entries were split into zones as follows: Europe 34; South America 10; Africa 28; Concacaf 15; Asia/Oceania 21. Israel was included in the European Zone. There were several subsequent withdrawals: Ghana and Uganda before playing in the first round, Libya before the second round, and Iran.

For the first time since 1958 Britain had more than one representative with England, Scotland and Northern Ireland qualifying. Wales and the Republic of Ireland only just failed to reach the finals on inferior goal difference.

The draw for the finals took place in Madrid, Spain on January 16, 1982. Spain as hosts, Argentina as holders, were seeded along with Italy, England, Brazil and West Germany – all the last five named being previous winners of the competition.

EUROPE

GROUP 1 (West Germany, Austria, Bulgaria, Finland, Albania)

4.6.80	Helsinki	**Finland v Bulgaria**	0-2 (0-1)
3.9.80	Tirana	**Albania v Finland**	2-0 (2-0)
24.9.80	Helsinki	**Finland v Austria**	0-2 (0-1)
19.10.80	Sofia	**Bulgaria v Albania**	2-1 (1-0)
15.11.80	Vienna	**Austria v Albania**	5-0 (3-0)
3.12.80	Sofia	**Bulgaria v West Germany**	1-3 (0-2)
6.12.80	Tirana	**Albania v Austria**	0-1 (0-1)
1.4.80	Tirana	**Albania v West Germany**	0-2 (0-1)
29.4.81	Hamburg	**West Germany v Austria**	2-0 (2-0)
13.5.81	Sofia	**Bulgaria v Finland**	4-0 (1-0)
24.5.81	Lahti	**Finland v West Germany**	0-4 (0-3)
28.5.81	Vienna	**Austria v Bulgaria**	2-0 (1-0)

17.6.81	Linz	**Austria v Finland**	5-1 (2-0)
2.9.81	Kotka	**Finland v Albania**	2-1 (0-0)
23.9.81	Bochum	**West Germany v Finland**	7-1 (2-1)
14.10.81	Vienna	**Austria v West Germany**	1-3 (1-2)
14.10.81	Tirana	**Albania v Bulgaria**	0-2 (0-0)
11.11.81	Sofia	**Bulgaria v Austria**	0-0 (0-0)
18.11.81	Dortmund	**West Germany v Albania**	8-0 (5-0)
22.11.81	Dusseldorf	**West Germany v Bulgaria**	4-0 (1-0)

	P	W	D	L	F	A	Pts
West Germany	8	8	0	0	33	3	16
Austria	8	5	1	2	16	6	11
Bulgaria	8	4	1	3	11	10	9
Albania	8	1	0	7	4	22	2
Finland	8	1	0	7	4	27	2

GROUP 2 (Netherlands, France Belgium, Eire, Cyprus)

26.3.80	Nicosia	**Cyprus v Eire**	2-3 (1-3)
10.9.80	Dublin	**Eire v Netherlands**	2-1 (0-0)
11.10.80	Limassol	**Cyprus v France**	0-7 (0-4)
15.10.80	Dublin	**Eire v Belgium**	1-1 (1-1)
28.10.80	Paris	**France v Eire**	2-0 (1-0)
19.11.80	Brussels	**Belgium v Netherlands**	1-0 (0-0)
19.11.80	Dublin	**Eire v Cyprus**	6-0 (4-0)
21.12.80	Nicosia	**Cyprus v Belgium**	0-2 (0-1)
18.2.81	Brussels	**Belgium v Cyprus**	3-2 (2-1)
22.2.81	Groningen	**Netherlands v Cyprus**	3-0 (1-0)
25.3.81	Rotterdam	**Netherlands v France**	1-0 (0-0)
25.3.81	Brussels	**Belgium v Eire**	1-0 (0-0)
29.4.81	Paris	**France v Belgium**	3-2 (3-1)
29.4.81	Nicosia	**Cyprus v Netherlands**	0-1 (0-1)
9.9.81	Rotterdam	**Netherlands v Eire**	2-2 (1-1)
9.9.81	Brussels	**Belgium v France**	2-0 (1-0)
14.10.81	Rotterdam	**Netherlands v Belgium**	3-0 (2-0)
14.10.81	Dublin	**Eire v France**	3-2 (3-1)
18.11.81	Paris	**France v Netherlands**	2-0 (0-0)
5.12.81	Paris	**France v Cyprus**	4-0 (2-0)

	P	W	D	L	F	A	Pts
Belgium	8	5	1	2	12	9	11
France	8	5	0	3	20	8	10
Eire	8	4	2	2	17	11	10
Netherlands	8	4	1	3	11	7	9
Cyprus	8	0	0	8	4	29	0

GROUP 3 (Czechoslovakia, USSR, Wales, Turkey, Iceland)

2.6.80	Reykjavik	**Iceland v Wales**	0-4 (0-1)
3.9.80	Reykjavik	**Iceland v USSR**	1-2 (0-1)
24.9.80	Izmir	**Turkey v Iceland**	1-3 (0-1)
15.10.80	Cardiff	**Wales v Turkey**	4-0 (2-0)

15.10.80	Moscow	**USSR v Iceland**	5-0 (2-0)
19.11.80	Cardiff	**Wales v Czechoslovakia**	1-0 (1-0)
3.12.80	Prague	**Czechoslovakia v Turkey**	2-0 (2-0)
25.3.81	Ankara	**Turkey v Wales**	0-1 (0-0)
15.4.81	Istanbul	**Turkey v Czechoslovakia**	0-3 (0-0)
27.5.81	Bratislava	**Czechoslovakia v Iceland**	6-1 (2-0)
30.5.81	Wrexham	**Wales v USSR**	0-0 (0-0)
9.9.81	Reykjavik	**Iceland v Turkey**	2-0 (1-0)
9.9.81	Prague	**Czechoslovakia v Wales**	2-0 (1-0)
23.9.81	Reykjavik	**Iceland v Czechoslovakia**	1-1 (1-0)
23.9.81	Moscow	**USSR v Turkey**	4-0 (3-0)
7.10.81	Izmir	**Turkey v USSR**	0-3 (0-2)
14.10.81	Swansea	**Wales v Iceland**	2-2 (1-0)
28.10.81	Tbilisi	**USSR v Czechoslovakia**	2-0 (1-0)
18.11.81	Tbilisi	**USSR v Wales**	3-0 (2-0)
29.11.81	Bratislava	**Czechoslovakia v USSR**	1-1 (1-1)

	P	W	D	L	F	A	Pts
USSR	8	6	2	0	20	2	14
Czechoslovakia	8	4	2	2	15	6	10
Wales	8	4	2	2	12	7	10
Iceland	8	2	2	4	10	21	6
Turkey	8	0	0	8	1	22	0

GROUP 4 (England, Hungary, Switzerland, Rumania, Norway)

10.9.80	Wembley	**England v Norway**	4-0 (1-0)
24.9.80	Oslo	**Norway v Rumania**	1-1 (1-1)
15.10.80	Bucharest	**Rumania v England**	2-1 (1-0)
29.10.80	Berne	**Switzerland v Norway**	1-2 (0-1)
19.11.80	Wembley	**England v Switzerland**	2-1 (2-0)
28.4.81	Lucerne	**Switzerland v Hungary**	2-2 (1-1)
29.4.81	Wembley	**England v Rumania**	0-0 (0-0)
13.5.81	Budapest	**Hungary v Rumania**	1-0 (1-0)
20.5.81	Oslo	**Norway v Hungary**	1-2 (0-0)
30.5.81	Basle	**Switzerland v England**	2-1 (2-0)
3.6.81	Bucharest	**Rumania v Norway**	1-0 (0-0)
6.6.81	Budapest	**Hungary v England**	1-3 (1-1)
17.6.81	Oslo	**Norway v Switzerland**	1-1 (0-0)
9.9.81	Oslo	**Norway v England**	2-1 (2-1)
23.9.81	Bucharest	**Rumania v Hungary**	0-0 (0-0)
10.10.81	Bucharest	**Rumania v Switzerland**	1-2 (0-0)
14.10.81	Budapest	**Hungary v Switzerland**	3-0 (1-0)
31.10.81	Budapest	**Hungary v Norway**	4-1 (1-1)
11.11.81	Berne	**Switzerland v Rumania**	0-0 (0-0)
18.11.81	Wembley	**England v Hungary**	1-0 (1-0)

	P	W	D	L	F	A	Pts
Hungary	8	4	2	2	13	8	10
England	8	4	1	3	13	8	9
Rumania	8	2	4	2	5	5	8

Switzerland	8	2	3	3	9	12	7
Norway	8	2	2	4	8	15	6

GROUP 5 (Italy, Yugoslavia, Greece, Denmark, Luxembourg)

10.9.80	Luxembourg	**Luxembourg v Yugoslavia**	0-5 (0-0)
27.9.80	Ljubljana	**Yugoslavia v Denmark**	2-1 (2-1)
11.10.80	Luxembourg	**Luxembourg v Italy**	0-2 (0-1)
15.10.80	Copenhagen	**Denmark v Greece**	0-1 (0-0)
1.11.80	Rome	**Italy v Denmark**	2-0 (1-0)
15.11.80	Turin	**Italy v Yugoslavia**	2-0 (1-0)
19.11.80	Copenhagen	**Denmark v Luxembourg**	4-0 (2-0)
6.12.80	Athens	**Greece v Italy**	0-2 (0-1)
28.1.81	Salonika	**Greece v Luxembourg**	2-0 (2-0)
11.3.81	Luxembourg	**Luxembourg v Greece**	0-2 (0-1)
29.4.81	Split	**Yugoslavia v Greece**	5-1 (3-0)
1.5.81	Luxembourg	**Luxembourg v Denmark**	1-2 (1-0)
3.6.81	Copenhagen	**Denmark v Italy**	3-1 (0-0)
9.9.81	Copenhagen	**Denmark v Yugoslavia**	1-2 (0-0)
14.10.81	Salonika	**Greece v Denmark**	2-3 (0-2)
17.10.81	Belgrade	**Yugoslavia v Italy**	1-1 (1-1)
14.11.81	Turin	**Italy v Greece**	1-1 (0-0)
21.11.81	Novi Sad	**Yugoslavia v Luxembourg**	5-0 (2-0)
29.11.81	Athens	**Greece v Yugoslavia**	1-2 (1-2)
5.12.81	Naples	**Italy v Luxembourg**	1-0 (1-0)

	P	**W**	**D**	**L**	**F**	**A**	**Pts**
Yugoslavia	8	6	1	1	22	7	13
Italy	8	5	2	1	12	5	12
Denmark	8	4	0	4	14	11	8
Greece	8	3	1	4	10	13	7
Luxembourg	8	0	0	8	1	23	0

GROUP 6 (Scotland, Sweden, Portugal, Northern Ireland, Israel)

26.3.80	Tel Aviv	**Israel v Northern Ireland**	0-0 (0-0)
18.6.80	Solna	**Sweden v Israel**	1-1 (1-0)
10.9.80	Solna	**Sweden v Scotland**	0-1 (0-0)
15.10.80	Belfast	**Northern Ireland v Sweden**	3-0 (3-0)
15.10.80	Glasgow	**Scotland v Portugal**	0-0 (0-0)
12.11.80	Tel Aviv	**Israel v Sweden**	0-0 (0-0)
19.11.80	Lisbon	**Portugal v Northern Ireland**	1-0 (0-0)
17.12.80	Lisbon	**Portugal v Israel**	3-0 (2-0)
25.2.81	Tel Aviv	**Israel v Scotland**	0-1 (0-0)
25.3.81	Glasgow	**Scotland v Northern Ireland**	1-1 (0-0)
28.4.81	Glasgow	**Scotland v Israel**	3-1 (2-0)
29.4.81	Belfast	**Northern Ireland v Portugal**	1-0 (0-0)
3.6.81	Solna	**Sweden v Northern Ireland**	1-0 (0-0)
24.6.81	Solna	**Sweden v Portugal**	3-0 (1-0)
9.9.81	Glasgow	**Scotland v Sweden**	2-0 (1-0)
14.10.81	Lisbon	**Portugal v Sweden**	1-2 (0-1)
14.10.81	Belfast	**Northern Ireland v Scotland**	0-0 (0-0)

28.10.81	Tel Aviv	**Israel v Portugal**	4-1 (4-1)
18.11.81	Belfast	**Northern Ireland v Israel**	1-0 (1-0)
18.11.81	Lisbon	**Portugal v Scotland**	2-1 (1-1)

	P	W	D	L	F	A	Pts
Scotland	8	4	3	1	9	4	11
Northern Ireland	8	3	3	2	6	3	9
Sweden	8	3	2	3	7	8	8
Portugal	8	3	1	4	8	11	7
Israel	8	1	3	4	6	10	5

GROUP 7 (Poland, East Germany, Malta)

7.12.80	Valletta	**Malta v Poland**	0-2 (0-0)*
4.4.81	Valletta	**Malta v East Germany**	1-2 (1-2)
2.5.81	Warsaw	**Poland v East Germany**	1-0 (0-0)
10.10.81	Leipzig	**East Germany v Poland**	2-3 (0-2)
11.11.81	Jena	**East Germany v Malta**	5-1 (2-1)
15.11.81	Wroclaw	**Poland v Malta**	6-0 (1-0)

*Match abandoned after 77 minutes through crowd interference but score allowed to stand.

	P	W	D	L	F	A	Pts
Poland	4	4	0	0	12	2	8
East Germany	4	2	0	2	9	6	4
Malta	4	0	0	4	2	15	0

SOUTH AMERICA

GROUP 1 (Brazil, Bolivia, Venezuela)

8.2.81	Caracas	**Venezuela v Brazil**	0-1 (0-0)
15.2.81	La Paz	**Bolivia v Venezuela**	3-0 (1-0)
22.2.81	La Paz	**Bolivia v Brazil**	1-2 (1-1)
15.3.81	Caracas	**Venezuela v Bolivia**	1-0 (1-0)
22.3.81	Rio de Janeiro	**Brazil v Bolivia**	3-1 (1-0)
29.3.81	Goiania	**Brazil v Venezuela**	5-0 (1-0)

	P	W	D	L	F	A	Pts
Brazil	4	4	0	0	11	2	8
Bolivia	4	1	0	3	5	6	2
Venezuela	4	1	0	3	1	9	2

GROUP 2 (Colombia, Peru, Uruguay)

26.7.81	Bogota	**Colombia v Peru**	1-1 (0-0)
9.8.81	Montevideo	**Uruguay v Colombia**	3-2 (1-1)
16.8.81	Lima	**Peru v Colombia**	2-0 (1-0)
23.8.81	Montevideo	**Uruguay v Peru**	1-2 (0-2)
6.9.81	Lima	**Peru v Uruguay**	0-0 (0-0)
13.9.81	Bogota	**Colombia v Uruguay**	1-1 (1-1)

	P	W	D	L	F	A	Pts
Peru	4	2	2	0	5	2	6
Uruguay	4	1	2	1	5	5	4
Colombia	4	0	2	2	4	7	2

Only Uruguay of the 6 previous World Cup winners failed to qualify for the 1982 finals in Spain. Yet the Uruguayans had won the Copa de Oro, a competition between previous World Cup winners held in Montevideo in 1981. Only England did not compete in this, their place being taken by the Netherlands, runners-up in the 1974 and 1978 World Cup finals.

GROUP 3 (Chile, Ecuador, Paraguay)

17.5.81	Guayaquil	**Ecuador v Paraguay**	1-0 (0-0)
24.5.81	Guayaquil	**Ecuador v Chile**	0-0 (0-0)
31.5.81	Asuncion	**Paraguay v Ecuador**	3-1 (0-0)
7.6.81	Asuncion	**Paraguay v Chile**	0-1 (0-0)
14.6.81	Santiago	**Chile v Ecuador**	2-0 (1-0)
21.6.81	Santiago	**Chile v Paraguay**	3-0 (3-0)

	P	W	D	L	F	A	Pts
Chile	4	3	1	0	6	0	7
Ecuador	4	1	1	2	2	5	3
Paraguay	4	1	0	3	3	6	2

AFRICA

1st ROUND (Tunisia, Nigeria, Uganda, Madagascar, Senegal, Morocco, Zaire, Mozambique, Cameroon, Malawi, Guinea, Lesotho, Libya, Gambia, Ethiopia, Zambia, Niger, Somalia, Sierra Leone, Algeria, Ghana, Egypt, Kenya, Tanzania. Zimbabwe, Sudan, Liberia and Togo byes to 2nd Round)

22.6.80	Dakar	**Senegal v Morocco**	0-1 (0-1)
6.7.80	Casablanca	**Morocco v Senegal**	0-0 (0-0)
13.7.80	Kinshasa	**Zaire v Mozambique**	5-2 (1-1)
27.7.80	Maputo	**Mozambique v Zaire**	1-2 (0-2)
29.6.80	Yaounde	**Cameroon v Malawi**	3-0 (1-0)
20.7.80	Kamusu	**Malawi v Cameroon**	1-1 (0-0)
22.6.80	Conakry	**Guinea v Lesotho**	3-1 (1-1)
6.7.80	Maseru	**Lesotho v Guinea**	1-1 (0-1)
29.6.80	Tunis	**Tunisia v Nigeria**	2-0 (1-0)
12.7.80	Lagos	**Nigeria v Tunisia**	2-0 (1-0)
			(Nigeria won 4-3 on penalty kicks)
8.5.80	Tripoli	**Libya v Gambia**	2-1 (1-0)
6.7.80	Banjul	**Gambia v Libya**	0-0 (0-0)
18.5.80	Addis Abeba	**Ethiopia v Zambia**	0-0 (0-0)
1.6.80	N'Dola	**Zambia v Ethiopia**	4-0 (2-0)

16.7.80	Niamey	**Niger v Somalia**	0-0 (0-0)
27.7.80	Mogadiscio	**Somalia v Niger**	1-1 (0-1)
31.5.80	Freetown	**Sierra Leone v Algeria**	2-2 (0-0)
13.6.80	Oran	**Algeria v Sierra Leone**	3-1 (1-0)
5.7.80	Nairobi	**Kenya v Tanzania**	3-1 (1-1)
19.7.80	Dar-es-Salaam	**Tanzania v Kenya**	5-0 (1-0)

Ghana v Egypt: Ghana withdrew 11.6.80; Egypt walked over to 2nd Round.

Uganda v Madagascar: Uganda withdrew 26.6.80; Madagascar walked over to 2nd Round.

2nd ROUND

12.12.80	Constantine	**Algeria v Sudan**	2-0 (2-0)
28.12.80	Khartoum	**Sudan v Algeria**	1-1 (0-0)
14.12.80	Niamey	**Niger v Togo**	0-1 (0-0)
28.12.80	Lome	**Togo v Niger**	1-2 (0-0)
7.12.80	Monrovia	**Liberia v Guinea**	0-0 (0-0)
21.12.80	Conakry	**Guinea v Liberia**	1-0 (1-0)
12.10.80	Douala	**Cameroon v Zimbabwe**	2-0 (0-0)
16.11.80	Salisbury	**Zimbabwe v Cameroon**	1-0 (1-0)
16.11.80	Fes	**Morocco v Zambia**	2-0 (2-0)
30.11.80	Lusaka	**Zambia v Morocco**	2-0 (0-0)
		(Morocco won 5-4 on penalty kicks)	
6.12.80	Lagos	**Nigeria v Tanzania**	1-1 (1-0)
20.12.80	Dar-es-Salaam	**Tanzania v Nigeria**	0-2 (0-1)
16.11.80	Tananarive	**Madagascar v Zaire**	1-1 (1-0)
21.12.80	Kinshasa	**Zaire v Madagascar**	3-2 (2-2)

Libya v Egypt: Libya withdrew 22.12.80; Egypt walked over to 3rd Round

3rd ROUND

1.5.81	Constantine	**Algeria v Niger**	4-0 (1-0)
31.5.81	Niamey	**Niger v Algeria**	1-0 (0-0)
12.4.81	Conakry	**Guinea v Nigeria**	1-1 (0-1)
25.4.81	Lagos	**Nigeria v Guinea**	1-0 (0-0)
26.4.81	Casablanca	**Morocco v Egypt**	1-0 (1-0)
8.5.81	Cairo	**Egypt v Morocco**	0-0 (0-0)
12.4.81	Kinshasa	**Zaire v Cameroon**	1-0 (1-0)
26.4.81	Yaounde	**Cameroon v Zaire**	6-1 (3-0)

FINAL MATCHES

10.10.81	Lagos	**Nigeria v Algeria**	0-2 (0-2)
30.10.81	Constantine	**Algeria v Nigeria**	2-1 (1-1)
15.11.81	Kenitra	**Morocco v Cameroon**	0-2 (0-2)
29.11.81	Yaounde	**Cameroon v Morocco**	2-1 (1-1)

Algeria and Cameroon qualified.

CONCACAF

NORTHERN ZONE (Canada, USA, Mexico)

18.10.80	Toronto	**Canada v Mexico**	1-1 (1-0)
25.10.80	Fort Lauderdale	**USA v Canada**	0-0 (0-0)
1.11.80	Vancouver	**Canada v USA**	2-1 (2-0)
9.11.80	Mexico City	**Mexico v USA**	5-1 (4-0)
16.11.80	Mexico City	**Mexico v Canada**	1-1 (0-0)
23.11.80	Fort Lauderdale	**USA v Mexico**	2-1 (1-1)

	P	W	D	L	F	A	Pts
Canada	4	1	3	0	4	3	5
Mexico	4	1	2	1	8	5	4
USA	4	1	1	2	4	8	3

Canada and Mexico qualified for Concacaf Final Tournament.

CENTRAL ZONE (Panama, Costa Rica, El Salvador, Guatemala, Honduras)

2.7.80	Panama City	**Panama v Guatemala**	0-2 (0-1)
30.7.80	Panama City	**Panama v Honduras**	0-2 (0-1)
10.8.80	Panama City	**Panama v Costa Rica**	1-1 (1-0)
24.8.80	Panama City	**Panama v El Salvador**	1-3 (0-1)
1.10.80	San Jose	**Costa Rica v Honduras**	2-3 (0-2)
5.10.80	San Salvador	**El Salvador v Panama**	4-1 (2-1)
12.10.80	Guatemala City	**Guatemala v Costa Rica**	0-0 (0-0)
26.10.80	Tegucigalpa	**Honduras v Guatemala**	0-0 (0-0)
26.10.80	San Salvador	**El Salvador v Costa Rica** not played; Costa Rica refused to play in El Salvador because of security reasons; match awarded 2-0 to El Salvador	
5.11.80	San Jose	**Costa Rica v Panama**	2-0 (1-0)
9.11.80	Guatemala City	**Guatemala v El Salvador**	0-0 (0-0)
16.11.80	Guatemala City	**Guatemala v Panama**	5-0 (2-0)
16.11.80	Tegucigalpa	**Honduras v Costa Rica**	1-1 (0-1)
23.11.80	San Salvador	**El Salvador v Honduras**	2-1 (1-0)
26.11.80	San Jose	**Costa Rica v Guatemala**	0-3 (0-1)
30.11.80	Tegucigalpa	**Honduras v El Salvador**	2-0 (1-0)
7.12.80	Guatemala City	**Guatemala v Honduras**	0-1 (0-0)
10.12.80	San Jose	**Costa Rica v El Salvador**	0-0 (0-0)
14.12.80	Tegucigalpa	**Honduras v Panama**	5-0 (3-0)
21.12.80	San Salvador	**El Salvador v Guatemala**	1-0 (0-0)

	P	W	D	L	F	A	Pts
Honduras	8	5	2	1	15	5	12
El Salvador	8	5	2	1	12	5	12
Guatemala	8	3	3	2	10	2	9
Costa Rica	8	1	4	3	6	10	6
Panama	8	0	1	7	3	24	1

Honduras and El Salvador qualified for Concacaf Final Tournament.

CARIBBEAN ZONE

EXTRA PRELIMINARY ROUND (Grenada, Guyana)

30.3.80	Georgetown	**Guyana v Grenada**	5-2 (2-2)
13.4.80	Grenada	**Grenada v Guyana**	2-3 (0-2)

GROUP A (Cuba, Surinam, Guyana)

17.8.80	Havana	**Cuba v Surinam**	3-0 (0-0)
7.9.80	Paramaribo	**Surinam v Cuba**	0-0 (0-0)
28.9.80	Georgetown	**Guyana v Surinam**	0-1 (0-1)
12.10.80	Paramaribo	**Surinam v Guyana**	4-0 (2-0)
9.11.80	Havana	**Cuba v Guyana**	1-0 (1-0)
30.11.80	Lynden	**Guyana v Cuba**	0-3 (0-3)

	P	W	D	L	F	A	Pts
Cuba	4	3	1	0	7	0	7
Surinam	4	2	1	1	5	3	5
Guyana	4	0	0	4	0	9	0

Cuba qualified for Concacaf Final Tournament.

GROUP B (Haiti, Trinidad and Tobago, Netherlands Antilles)

1.8.80	Port au Prince	**Haiti v Trinidad–Tobago**	2-0 (0-0)
17.8.80	San Fernando	**Trinidad–Tobago v Haiti**	1-0 (0-0)
12.9.80	Port au Prince	**Haiti v Netherlands Antilles**	1-0 (0-0)
9.11.80	Port of Spain	**Trinidad–Tobago v Netherlands Antilles**	0-0 (0-0)
29.11.80	Curacao	**Netherlands Antilles v Trinidad–Tobago**	0-0 (0-0)
12.12.80	Curacao	**Netherlands Antilles v Haiti**	1-1 (0-1)

	P	W	D	L	F	A	Pts
Haiti	4	2	1	1	4	2	5
Trinidad-Tobago	4	1	2	1	1	2	4
Netherlands Antilles	4	0	3	1	1	2	3

Haiti qualified for Concacaf Final Tournament.

CONCACAF FINAL TOURNAMENT IN TEGUCIGALPA, HONDURAS

1.11.81	Tegucigalpa	**Mexico v Cuba**	4-0 (2-0)
2.11.81	Tegucigalpa	**Canada v El Salvador**	1-0 (0-0)
3.11.81	Tegucigalpa	**Honduras v Haiti**	4-0 (2-0)
6.11.81	Tegucigalpa	**Haiti v Canada**	1-1 (1-0)
6.11.81	Tegucigalpa	**Mexico v El Salvador**	0-1 (0-0)
8.11.81	Tegucigalpa	**Honduras v Cuba**	2-0 (1-0)
11.11.81	Tegucigalpa	**El Salvador v Cuba**	0-0 (0-0)
11.11.81	Tegucigalpa	**Mexico v Haiti**	1-1 (0-0)
12.11.81	Tegucigalpa	**Honduras v Canada**	2-1 (2-1)
15.11.81	Tegucigalpa	**Haiti v Cuba**	0-2 (0-0)
15.11.81	Tegucigalpa	**Mexico v Canada**	1-1 (1-0)
16.11.81	Tegucigalpa	**Honduras v El Salvador**	0-0 (0-0)
19.11.81	Tegucigalpa	**Haiti v El Salvador**	0-1 (0-1)

22.11.81	Tegucigalpa	**Cuba v Canada**	2-2 (1-0)
22.11.81	Tegucigalpa	**Honduras v Mexico**	0-0 (0-0)

	P	W	D	L	F	A	Pts
Honduras	5	3	2	0	8	1	8
El Salvador	5	2	2	1	2	1	6
Mexico	5	1	3	1	6	3	5
Canada	5	1	3	1	6	6	5
Cuba	5	1	2	2	4	8	4
Haiti	5	0	2	3	2	9	2

ASIA/OCEANIA

GROUP 1 (Indonesia, Australia, Fiji, New Zealand, Taiwan)

25.4.81	Auckland	**New Zealand v Australia**	3-3 (2-3)
3.5.81	Suva	**Fiji v New Zealand**	0-4 (0-3)
7.5.81	Taipei	**Taiwan v New Zealand**	0-0 (0-0)
11.5.81	Djakarta	**Indonesia v New Zealand**	0-2 (0-1)
16.5.81	Sydney	**Australia v New Zealand**	0-2 (0-1)
20.5.81	Melbourne	**Australia v Indonesia**	2-0 (2-0)
23.5.81	Auckland	**New Zealand v Indonesia**	5-0 (2-0)
30.5.81	Auckland	**New Zealand v Taiwan**	2-0 (1-0)
31.5.81	Suva	**Fiji v Indonesia**	0-0 (0-0)
6.6.81	Suva	**Fiji v Taiwan**	2-1 (1-0)
10.6.81	Melbourne	**Australia v Taiwan**	3-2 (1-0)
15.6.81	Djakarta	**Indonesia v Taiwan**	1-0 (0-0)
28.6.81	Taipei	**Taiwan v Indonesia**	2-0 (2-0)
26.7.81	Suva	**Fiji v Australia**	1-4 (0-4)
4.8.81	Taipei	**Taiwan v Fiji**	0-0 (0-0)
10.8.81	Djakarta	**Indonesia v Fiji**	3-3 (3-1)
14.8.81	Melbourne	**Australia v Fiji**	10-0 (3-0)
16.8.81	Auckland	**New Zealand v Fiji**	13-0 (7-0)
30.8.81	Djakarta	**Indonesia v Australia**	1-0 (0-0)
6.9.81	Taipei	**Taiwan v Australia**	0-0 (0-0)

	P	W	D	L	F	A	Pts
New Zealand	8	6	2	0	31	3	14
Australia	8	4	2	2	22	9	10
Indonesia	8	2	2	4	5	14	6
Taiwan	8	1	3	4	5	8	5
Fiji	8	1	3	4	6	35	5

New Zealand qualified for Asia/Oceania Final Tournament.

Fiji created history when they lost 13-0 to New Zealand in a 1982 qualifying match. It was a record score for the competition. Two days earlier they had lost 10-0 to Australia.

GROUP 2 (Iraq, Syria, Bahrain, Qatar, Saudi Arabia)

Tournament in Riyadh, Saudi Arabia

18.3.81	Riyadh	**Qatar v Iraq**	0-1 (0-0)
19.3.81	Riyadh	**Syria v Bahrain**	0-1 (0-0)
21.3.81	Riyadh	**Iraq v Saudi Arabia**	0-1 (0-0)
22.3.81	Riyadh	**Qatar v Bahrain**	3-0 (2-0)
24.3.81	Riyadh	**Syria v Saudi Arabia**	0-2 (0-0)
25.3.81	Riyadh	**Iraq v Bahrain**	2-0 (1-0)
27.3.81	Riyadh	**Qatar v Syria**	2-1 (1-0)
28.3.81	Riyadh	**Bahrain v Saudi Arabia**	0-1 (0-0)
30.3.81	Riyadh	**Iraq v Syria**	2-1 (1-0)
31.3.81	Riyadh	**Qatar v Saudi Arabia**	0-1 (0-0)

	P	W	D	L	F	A	Pts
Saudi Arabia	4	4	0	0	5	0	8
Iraq	4	3	0	1	5	2	6
Qatar	4	2	0	2	5	3	4
Bahrain	4	1	0	3	1	6	2
Syria	4	0	0	4	2	7	0

Saudi Arabia qualified for Asia/Oceania Final Tournament.

GROUP III (Kuwait, Thailand, Malaysia, South Korea, Iran)

Iran withdrew 17.3.81

Tournament in Kuwait

21.4.81	Kuwait	**Malaysia v South Korea**	1-2 (1-1)
22.4.81	Kuwait	**Kuwait v Thialand**	6-0 (4-0)
24.4.81	Kuwait	**South Korea v Thailand**	5-1 (2-1)
25.4.81	Kuwait	**Kuwait v Malaysia**	4-0 (2-0)
27.4.81	Kuwait	**Malaysia v Thailand**	2-2 (0-0)
29.4.81	Kuwait	**Kuwait v South Korea**	2-0 (0-0)

	P	W	D	L	F	A	Pts
Kuwait	3	3	0	0	12	0	6
South Korea	3	2	0	1	7	4	4
Malaysia	3	0	1	2	3	8	1
Thailand	3	0	1	2	3	13	1

Kuwait qualified for Asia/Oceania Final Tournament.

GROUP IV (Hong Kong, Macao, China, North Korea, Japan, Singapore)

Tournament in Hong Kong

Play-off matches

21.12.80	Hong Kong	**Hong Kong v China**	0-1 (0-0)
22.12.80	Hong Kong	**North Korea v Macao**	3-0 (2-0)
22.12.80	Hong Kong	**Singapore v Japan**	0-1 (0-1)

Group A

24.12.80	Hong Kong	**China v Macao**	3-0 (2-0)
26.12.80	Hong Kong	**China v Japan**	1-0 (1-0)
28.12.80	Hong Kong	**Japan v Macao**	3-0 (0-0)

Group B

24.12.80	Hong Kong	**Hong Kong v Singapore**	1-1 (0-0)
26.12.80	Hong Kong	**Singapore v North Korea**	0-1 (0-1)
28.12.80	Hong Kong	**Hong Kong v North Korea**	2-2 (1-2)

Semi-finals

30.12.80	Hong Kong	**North Korea v Japan**	1-0 (0-0)
31.12.80	Hong Kong	**China v Hong Kong**	0-0 (0-0)

(China won 5-4 on penalty kicks)

Final

4.1.81	Hong Kong	**China v North Korea**	4-2 (1-1)

(after extra time)

China qualified for Asia/Oceania Final Tournament.

FINAL TOURNAMENT

24.9.81	Peking	**China v New Zealand**	0-0 (0-0)
3.10.81	Auckland	**New Zealand v China**	1-0 (1-0)
10.10.81	Auckland	**New Zealand v Kuwait**	1-2 (1-0)
18.10.81	Peking	**China v Kuwait**	3-0 (2-0)
4.11.81	Riyadh	**Saudi Arabia v Kuwait**	0-1 (0-0)
12.11.81	Kuala Lumpur	**Saudi Arabia v China**	2-4 (2-0)
19.11.81	Kuala Lumpur	**China v Saudi Arabia**	2-0 (2-0)
28.11.81	Auckland	**New Zealand v Saudi Arabia**	2-2 (2-1)
30.11.81	Kuwait	**Kuwait v China**	1-0 (1-0)
7.12.81	Kuwait	**Kuwait v Saudi Arabia**	2-0 (1-0)
14.12.81	Kuwait	**Kuwait v New Zealand**	2-2 (1-0)
19.12.81	Riyadh	**Saudi Arabia v New Zealand**	0-5 (0-5)

	P	W	D	L	F	A	Pts
Kuwait	6	4	1	1	8	6	9
New Zealand	6	2	3	1	11	6	7
China	6	3	1	2	9	4	7
Saudi Arabia	6	0	1	5	4	16	1

Play-off

10.1.82	Singapore	**New Zealand v China**	2-1 (1-0)

West Germany were the only all-winning team in the 1982 qualifying matches. Thus they maintained their record of never losing a qualifying game in the competition.

1982 Game-By-Game Record Cards

Jack Rollin's game-by-game record cards have been designed to enable you to participate in the 52 World Cup matches as they are played in Spain. Once completed, they provide a unique, personalised record of the 1982 Cup and, with the rest of the book, the fullest record of World Cup history to date.

First phase
Group 3

Argentina 0 1 **Belgium**

[ ]

13 June
Barcelona/Nou Camp

No.	Argentina	Belgium	No.

Scorers

Substitutes

Referee Linesmen

14 June
Vigo/Balaidos

Italy 0 0 **Poland**

[0 I 0]

First phase
Group 1

No.			No.

Scorers

Substitutes

Referee Linesmen

14 June
Seville/S. Pizjuan

Brazil 2 1 **USSR**

[I]

First phase
Group 6

No.			No.

Scorers

Substitutes

Referee Linesmen

First phase
Group 1

Peru 0 : 0 **Cameroon**

[0 : 0]

15 June
La Coruna/Riazor

No.			No.

Scorers

Substitutes

Referee Linesmen

First phase
Group 3

Hungary 10 : 1 **El Salvador**

[:]

15 June
Elche/Nuevo Estadio

No.			No.

Scorers

Substitutes

Referee Linesmen

15 June
Málaga/La Rosaleda

Scotland 5 | 2 **New Zealand**

First phase
Group 6

No.			No.

Scorers

	WOODDIN

Substitutes

Referee Linesmen

16 June
Gijon/El Molinon

West Germany 1 | 2 **Algeria**

First phase
Group 2

No.			No.

Scorers

	BELLOUMI (10)

Substitutes

Referee Linesmen

First phase
Group 4

England 3 [1] – [1] 1 France

16 June
Bilbao/San Mames

No.			No.

Scorers

ROBSON (16) (TWO) MARINER	SOLER (20)

Substitutes

Referee Linesmen

First phase
Group 5

Spain 1 [ ] – [ ] 1 Honduras

16 June
Valencia/Casanova

No.			No.

Scorers

Substitutes

Referee Linesmen

17 June
Oviedo/C. Tartiere

Chile 0 1 **Austria**

[I]

First phase
Group 2

No.			No.

Scorers

Substitutes

Referee Linesmen

17 June
Valladolid/Nuevo Zorrilla

Czechoslovakia 1 1 **Kuwait**

[I]

First phase
Group 4

No.			No.

Scorers

	FAISAL-AL-DAKHEEL (16)

Substitutes

Referee Linesmen

First phase
Group 5

Yugoslavia 0 0 **N. Ireland**

[0 0]

17 June
Zaragoza/La Romareda

No.			No.

Scorers

Substitutes

Referee Linesmen

First phase
Group 1

Italy 1 1 **Peru**

[ ]

18 June
Vigo/Balaidos

No.			No.

Scorers

Substitutes

Referee Linesmen

18 June
Alicante/Rico Perez

Argentina 4 | 1 **Hungary**

[|]

First phase
Group 3

No.			No.

Scorers

Substitutes

Referee Linesmen

18 June
Seville/B. Villamarin

Brazil 4 | 1 **Scotland**

[1 | 1]

First phase
Group 6

No.			No.

Scorers

ZICO(10) OSCAR(3) EDER(11) FALCÃO(15)	NAREY(14)

Substitutes

Referee Linesmen

First phase
La Coruna/Riazor

Poland 0 0 **Cameroon**

[0 0]

19 June
Group 1

No.			No.

Scorers

Substitutes

Referee Linesmen

First phase
Elche/Nuevo Estadio

Belgium 1 0 **El Salvador**

[ ]

19 June
Group 3

No.			No.

Scorers

Substitutes

Referee Linesmen

19 June
Málaga/La Rosaleda

USSR 5 2 **New Zealand**

[I]

First phase
Group 6

No.			No.

Scorers

Substitutes

Referee Linesmen

20 June
Gijon/El Molinon

West Germany 4 1 **Chile**

[I]

First phase
Group 2

No.			No.

Scorers

Substitutes

Referee Linesmen

First phase
Group 4

England 2 0 **Czechoslovakia**

20 June
Bilbao/San Mames

No.			No.

Scorers

Substitutes

Referee Linesmen

First phase
Group 5

Spain 2 1 **Yugoslavia**

20 June
Valencia/Casanova

No.			No.

Scorers

Substitutes

Referee Linesmen

21 June
Oviedo/C. Tartiere

Algeria 0 2 **Austria**

[I]

First phase
Group 2

No.			No.

Scorers

Substitutes

Referee Linesmen

21 June
Valladolid/Nuevo Zorrilla

France 4 1 **Kuwait**

[I]

First phase
Group 4

No.			No.

Scorers

Substitutes

Referee Linesmen

First phase
Group 5

Honduras 1 – 1 **N. Ireland**

[I]

21 June
Zaragoza/La Romareda

No.			No.

Scorers

	ARMSTRONG(9)

Substitutes

Referee Linesmen

First phase
Group 1

Peru 1 – 5 **Poland**

[I]

22 June
La Coruna/Riazor

No.			No.

Scorers

Substitutes

Referee Linesmen

22 June
Elche/Nuevo Estadio

Belgium 1 1 **Hungary**

[ ]

First phase
Group 3

No.			No.

Scorers

Substitutes

Referee Linesmen

22 June
Málaga/La Rosaleda

USSR 2 2 **Scotland**

[0 1]

First phase
Group 6

No.			No.

Scorers

CHIVADZE (3) SHENGALIA (7)	JORDAN (15) SOUNESS (4)

Substitutes

Referee Linesmen

First phase
Group 1

Italy 1 1 Cameroon

23 June
Vigo/Balaidos

[ ]

No.			No.

Scorers

Substitutes

Referee Linesmen

First phase
Group 3

Argentina 2 0 El Salvador

23 June
Alicante/Rico Perez

[ ]

No.			No.

Scorers

Substitutes

Referee Linesmen

23 June
Seville/Villamarin

Brazil 4 0 **New Zealand**

[I]

First phase
Group 6

No.			No.

Scorers

Substitutes

Referee Linesmen

24 June
Oviedo/C. Tartiere

Algeria 3 2 **Chile**

[I]

First phase
Group 2

No.			No.

Scorers

Substitutes

Referee Linesmen

First phase
Group 4

France — **Czechoslovakia**

24 June
Valladolid/Nuevo Zorrilla

No. | No.

Scorers

Substitutes

Referee — Linesmen

First phase
Group 5

Honduras — **Yugoslavia**

24 June
Zaragoza/La Romareda

No. | No.

Scorers

Substitutes

Referee — Linesmen

25 June
Gijon/El Molinon

West Germany 1 0 **Austria**

[ ]

First phase
Group 2

No.			No.

Scorers

Substitutes

Referee Linesmen

25 June
Bilbao/San Mames

England **Kuwait**

[ ]

First phase
Group 4

No.			No.

Scorers

Substitutes

Referee Linesmen

First phase
Group 5

Spain 0 1 **N. Ireland**
(0 0)

25 June
Valencia/Casanova

No.			No.

Scorers

	ARMSTRONG(9)

Substitutes

Referee   Linesmen

First phase table of results

Group 1	**P**	**W**	**D**	**L**	**F**	**A**	**Pts**
Italy	3	0	3	0	2	2	3
Poland	3	1	2	0	5	1	4
Peru	3	0	2	1	2	6	2
Cameroon	3	0	3	0	1	1	3

Group 3	**P**	**W**	**D**	**L**	**F**	**A**	**Pts**
Argentina	3	2	0	1	6	2	4
Belgium	3	2	1	0	3	1	5
Hungary	3	1	1	1	12	6	3
El Salvador	3	0	0	3	1	13	0

Group 6	**P**	**W**	**D**	**L**	**F**	**A**	**Pts**
Brazil	3	3	0	0	10	2	6
USSR	3	1	1	1	6	4	3
Scotland	3	1	1	0	8	8	3
New Zealand	3	0	0	3	2	12	0

Group 2	P	W	D	L	F	A	Pts
West Germany	3	2	0	1	6	3	4
Algeria	3	2	0	1	5	5	4
Chile	3	0	0	3	3	8	0
Austria	3	2	0	1	3	1	4

Group 4	P	W	D	L	F	A	Pts
England	3	3	0	0			6
France	3	2	0	1	6	5	4
Czechoslovakia	3	0	2	0	2	2	2
Kuwait	3	0	1	2			1

Group 5	P	W	D	L	F	A	Pts
Spain	3	1	1	0	3	3	3
Yugoslavia	3	0	2	1	2	3	2
N. Ireland	3	1	2	0	2	1	4
Honduras	3	0	3	0	3	3	3

For Second Phase fixtures, see page 8

28 June
Madrid/Calderon

AUSTRIA | 0 | 1 | FRANCE

[I]

Second phase
Section D

No.			No.

Scorers

Substitutes

Referee Linesmen

Second phase POLAND **3 0** BELGIUM **28 June**
Section A [I] **Barcelona/Nou Camp**

No.			No.

Scorers

Substitutes

Referee Linesmen

Second phase ITALY **2 1** ARGENTINA **29 June**
Section C [I] **Barcelona/Sarria**

No.			No.

Scorers

Substitutes

Referee Linesmen

29 June
Madrid/Bernabeu

Second phase
Section B

W. GERMANY 0 0 ENGLAND
[0 0]

No.			No.

Scorers

Substitutes

Referee Linesmen

1 July
Madrid/Calderon

Second phase
Section D

N. IRELAND 2 2 AUSTRIA
[ ]

No.			No.

Scorers

HAMILTON (11) (TWO)	

Substitutes

Referee Linesmen

Second phase USSR **1 0** BELGIUM **1 July**
Section A **Barcelona/Nou Camp**

[ ]

No.			No.

Scorers

Substitutes

Referee Linesmen

Second phase BRAZIL **3 0** ARGENTINA **2 July**
Section C **Barcelona/Sarria**

[ ]

No.			No.

Scorers

Substitutes

Referee Linesmen

2 July **Second phase**
~~Barcelona~~/Bernabeu **Section B**
MADRID

SPAIN [1] [2] W. GERMANY
[ ]

No.			No.

Scorers

Substitutes

Referee Linesmen

4 July **Second phase**
Madrid/Calderon **Section D**

N. IRELAND [1] [4] FRANCE
[0 1]

No.			No.

Scorers

ARMSTRONG (9)	GIRESSE (12) (TWO) ROCHETEAU (18) (TWO)

Substitutes

Referee Linesmen

Second phase
Section A

USSR 0 0 POLAND

[0 0]

4 July
Barcelona/Nou Camp

No.			No.

Scorers

Substitutes

Referee Linesmen

Second phase
Section C

BRAZIL 2 3 ITALY

[1 2]

5 July
Barcelona/Sarria

No.			No.
		ZOFF	1

Scorers

SOCRATES (8) FALCÃO (15)	ROSSI (20) (THREE)

Substitutes

Referee Linesmen

5 July
Madrid/Bernabeu SPAIN 0 0 ENGLAND

0 0

Second phase
Section B

No. No.

Scorers

Substitutes KEEGAN

Referee Linesmen

Second phase table of results

Section A	P	W	D	L	F	A	Pts
POLAND	2	1	1	0	3	0	3
USSR	2	1	1	0	1	0	3
BELGIUM	2	0	0	2	0	4	0

Section C	P	W	D	L	F	A	Pts
ITALY	2	2	0	0	5	3	4
BRAZIL	2	1	0	1	5	3	2
ARGENTINA	2	0	0	2	1	5	0

Section B	P	W	D	L	F	A	Pts
W. GERMANY	2	1	1	0	2	1	3
ENGLAND	2	0	2	0	0	0	2
SPAIN	2	0	1	1	1	2	1

Section D	P	W	D	L	F	A	Pts
FRANCE	2	2	0	0	5	1	4
N. IRELAND	2	0	1	1	3	6	1
AUSTRIA	2	0	1	1	3	3	1

Semi-final 8 July

POLAND 0 2 ITALY Barcelona/Nou Camp

[0 1]

No.			No.

Scorers

	ROSSI (20) (TWO)

Substitutes

Referee Linesmen

Semi-final 8 July

W. GERMANY 3 3 FRANCE Seville/S. Pizjuan

[1 1]

No.			No.
1	SCHUMACHER		22

Scorers

LITTBARSKI (7) RUMMENIGGE (11) FISCHER (8)	PLATINI (10) (PEN) TRESOR (8) GIRESSE (12)

Substitutes

BATTISTON

Referee Linesmen

W. GERMANY WIN ON PENALTIES (5-4) A.E.T

10 July **3rd/4th place**

Alicante/Rico Perez POLAND [3] [2] FRANCE

[|]

No.			No.

Scorers

Substitutes

Referee Linesmen

11 July **Final**

Madrid/Bernabeu ITALY [3] [1] W. GERMANY

[0 | 0]

No.			No.
1	ZOFF	SCHUMACHER	1

Scorers

ROSSI (20) TARDELLI, (14) ALTOBELLI	BREITNER (3)

Substitutes

Referee COELHO (BRAZIL) Linesmen

WIN great CASH PRIZES in DER's exclusive WORLD CUP TREASURE HUNT

Jack Rollin has devised 10 World Cup teasers, the answers to which are to be found in the pages of his book:

When in doubt, the book is right. All you have to do is write down the answers in the spaces provided, then suggest your ideal *British* World Cup team.

1. How many goals were scored in the 1982 qualifying competition?

Answer 1:

2. Which team scored the highest number of goals in the 1982 qualifying competition?

Answer 2:

3. Which World Cup Final match produced its first penalty goal?

Answer 3:

4. What is the total number of goals scored in all 11 World Cup Final matches?

Answer 4:

5. Which player achieved a hat-trick in a World Cup Final match?

Answer 5:

6. Which player scored the highest number of goals recorded in one World Cup final (i.e. post-qualifying) tournament, and give his individual total?

Answer 6:

7. What connection has the character in a book by Mary Shelley to do with 2 World Cup qualifying games played before World War II?

Answer 7:

8. In the first 11 World Cup final tournaments (i.e. all post-qualifying matches), what was the total number of goals scored?

Answer 8:

9. Only 1 country has won the World Cup while playing in a continent foreign to its own. Name it.

Answer 9:

10. In which World Cup was a qualifying competition first held?

Answer 10:

All questions relate to the eleven World Cup final tournaments (up to and including 1978) unless otherwise stated.

Treasure Hunt tie-breaker

Select your best British team (eleven names) from players who have previously appeared in a World Cup final tournament. This means picking England players from any of the 1950, 1954, 1958, 1962, 1966 and 1970 Cups; Northern Ireland and Wales from 1958 and Scotland from 1954, 1958, 1974 and 1978. It must be truly representative of all four countries but reflect the relative success of their team's performances. It can be listed as 2-3-5, 4-2-4, 4-3-3 or 4-4-2 after the goalkeeper chosen.

Then send your entry to:

The DER World Cup Treasure Hunt,
59 Charlotte Street,
London, W1P 1LA

The competition closes on Monday July 19, 1982, after which no entry forms will be accepted. Jack Rollin and DER will make the awards by the first post on Monday August 9, and their judgement is final.

First prize	**£1,000**
Second prize	**£500**
Third prize	**£250**
Fourth prize	**£250**

Name: ....

Address: ....

....

....

A list of winners will be available on request to anyone sending s.a.e. to the above address.